Praise for

Brand: It ain't the logo*

"Marketing is going digital. Customers and prospects are interacting with Brands in ways we never anticipated. It is up close and personal...and there is nowhere to hide. Understanding a Brand's equity, and delivering it consistently on-line, is a whole new challenge for marketers. Failure is everywhere – but Ted Matthews' book is an excellent, easy-to-read roadmap to success in this future."

Tony Miller

Former CEO MacLaren McCann and
Vice Chairman of McCann Worldgroup

"From Bangkok to Beijing and Sydney to Singapore, Ted's advice rings true because the Branding principles he so clearly articulates are universal. This makes Brand: It ain't the logo* (*It's what people think of you) *a must-read for marketing success in any hard-fought international arena."*

Ron McEachern

Past President, PepsiCo Asia

"This is really a book about organizational culture. Ted Matthews teaches us that 'the only synonym for Brand is culture' and that if you want to have a Brand that resonates with all types of stakeholders, inside and outside an organization, you need to go to work on building a strong and inspiring culture. This is the recipe for success in today's marketplace."

Lisa Zangari

Senior Vice President, Human Resources, IAMGOLD

"Ted Matthews wraps a persuasive argument in a lively read. This book is packed with fascinating examples that back up its clear-sighted analysis of how to build your Brand, and – just as important – how not to.

If you want highfalutin academic analysis, look elsewhere. But if you want clear, convincing and actionable advice on how to build your Brand, you've come to the right place."

Jim McElgunn

nior Editor, PROFIT Magazine

Praise for
Brand: It ain't the logo*

"Ted Matthews is the smartest brand specialist I know, and Brand: It ain't the logo* is the best, clearest, most sensible guide to the subject around. As branding plays an increasingly important role in an ever more competitive world, this is the book you need to build a better business."

Bo Burlingham

Author, *Small Giants: Companies that Choose to be Great Instead of Big*
Editor-at-Large, Inc. Magazine

"Brand: It ain't the logo* (*It's what people think of you) is a great read. I couldn't put it down. Great stories and great insights. I plan to lay it on our MBAs to help them in GettingItDone!"

Brendan Calder

Professor, GettingItDone, Rotman School of Management, University of Toronto

"Marketing has a handful of essential truths and I can think of nothing more essential than Ted's oft-repeated mantra that a Brand is 'what people think of you.' Ted's ability to cut through the clutter and deliver a message that sticks is legendary. It has been a joy to learn from him."

Ashwin W. Joshi

Director, MBA Program, Associate Professor in Marketing, Schulich School of Business, York University

"The battle for top talent is heating up in North America as more and more baby boomers retire and there are nowhere near enough skilled workers to replace them. If you want to attract, retain and inspire great people, you need to clearly define who you are, what you stand for and what difference you make – exactly what Matthews outlines in Brand: It ain't the logo* (*It's what people think of you). *Frankly speaking, this is the best book on Branding that I've ever read."*

Gabriel Bouchard

Former President and Chief Brand Officer, Workopolis

"Ted's lessons, 3 tools and 3 rules can be applied to any organization. Whether you have an established culture or an emerging one, read this book."

John Warrillow

Author, *Built to Sell: Creating a Business That Can Thrive Without You*

Brand

It ain't the logo*

*It's what people think of you™

---

ted matthews
with andris pone

Published by Instinct Brand Equity Coaches Inc.
Originally published in slightly different form in 2007 by Lulu.com

Fourth printing May 2012

Designed by Sol Studios | Todd De Koker
Cover image by Giant Vision | Andre Van Vugt

Special thanks to Kate Minden-Webb
for her research and market analysis smarts,
and for her tireless project leadership.

ISBN 9781477698525

For more Brand-building tools and resources, visit
www.instinctbrandequity.com

*Dedicated to my father Edwin, my entrepreneurial source code.
And to the devoted women in our lives who lived with and consistently
supported this oft-times affliction: Barbara – Edwin's wife and my
mother – and Marsha, my wife and mother of our children.*

Table of Contents

Brand Foundation Elements

Core Purpose – *Why we exist.*

Vision – *Where we are going, and how we'll know we're there.*

Mission – *What we do every day to get there.*

Values – *What we believe in; our principles.*

Position – *How we make a difference.*

Positioning Statement – *How we say our difference.*

Character – *How we act; our voice.*

Foreword

Who, in our world of hyper-messaging, has time for a Foreword? Let's get right into Chapter 1.

Ted Matthews

[1]   The Three Threats

It took me the better part of a 37-year career in marketing communications to convince myself that my definition of Brand was the right one – and to start convincing others.

"It's the biggest story of your lifetime. Because it's on your watch that this is happening. It's our generation that is witnessing the end of Western predominance."

Niall Ferguson

Sometimes I wish I'd done my career the other way around.

Before launching Instinct Brand Coaches in 2001, I spent the first three decades of my working life running the marketing company I founded, Promanad Communications. I enjoyed those years immensely. However, we could have used our resources – and our clients could have used theirs – much more effectively.

If only we'd all understood what a "Brand" truly was.

In 1971, after studying at the Ontario College of Art, I started up Promanad with my father. Coming from a design background, I tended to think of Brand the same way that my client CEOs and all the ad agencies did – as mainly a matter of "creative," the industry term that describes the ideas, words and design behind marketing and advertising materials. In other words, I believed, just like almost everybody else, that a Brand consisted mostly of a logo and advertising.

Even so, I tried to convince my clients that all of their marketing and advertising campaigns had to be built on a powerful communication device I called a "core idea." Core ideas, like TD's green chair, Maytag's lonely repairman or Subway's Jared (the guy who lost 200 pounds eating hoagies), express the unique positions of their Brands in ways that are relevant and compelling to the target audience.

It's vital that core ideas can stand the test of time, because if you want to keep your Brand in a customer's head, you had better first, tell them something real and essential about your Brand, and second, be consistent and not change the message all the time. Otherwise, people won't know what to think of your Brand from one day to the next.

The Challenge

Consistently communicate the core idea. For a variety of reasons, it was an almost impossible discipline to drive through client organizations when Promanad was growing in the 1970s and 80s. The main culprit was that, ironically, the ad agencies were then at the height of their power. They were in a position, quite the opposite of today, to easily deliver big sales increases for their clients.

Television typified how relatively straightforward it was. We lived in a universe of 13 channels, not hundreds. Because there were fewer ways to distribute corporate messaging, and because the overall pace of life was slower, customer attention wasn't nearly as fragmented as it is today. Relatively focused customer attention meant that advertisers just ran their spots to the huge audiences provided by the main networks, and the sales came rolling in.

The Tyranny of New Ideas

If a given campaign didn't work as well as expected, it was no big deal. Renewed success was as easy as the next new idea, creating a cavalier attitude among the ad agencies and their clients – which was, in fact, one of the main reasons that good campaigns failed in the first place. They weren't given time to take root, because the ad agencies and their clients were constantly rolling out new advertising with new core ideas – or with no core ideas at all.

Corporate Amnesia

Then there were the inevitable and increasingly common personnel changes that have become a part of doing business. Even if we did manage to focus the mind of a client on communicating a consistent core idea, our contacts within the organization would eventually move on, and that organization's commitment to working on consistent Brand communications went out the door with them. There was simply no corporate memory.

Consistency was almost impossible to drive through client organizations.

The people who replaced them, quite naturally, came into their new jobs with a burning desire to prove themselves. But people don't typically set out to prove themselves by simply perpetuating the ideas of those who came before them. These "new friends" inside the Brand organization discard the ideas of their predecessors – often, even if the ideas were working beautifully – and insist on their own new program in a bid to make their mark.

And so the client would direct us to abandon the "old" ideas and work on something new. We would grudgingly turn our backs on all the time that was spent developing those ideas, abandon any momentum that may have been built up in the target audience, and start all over again.

Kill the Bunny?

Complicit with the Brand's new friends were its "old friends" – the people on the client side who were bored or had even grown hateful of the Brand message and were willing to do something, anything, to change it. Eventually it happens in every organization. I had Energizer batteries as a client for several years and every year we'd have a meeting to work on their strategy for selling through retail stores. Not a single meeting went by without one of the Energizer execs pleading with me: "Do we have to use that damn bunny again?"

Luckily we managed to convince them, year in and year out, to stick with the bunny. So the Energizer folks became an exception when it came to understanding the importance of consistency. They were able to suppress their murderous urges because the bunny – a powerful core idea – was such a runaway winner.

The "Aha" Moment

Old friends and new friends kept our clients' Brand communications in a constant state of flux. I wondered: how will stakeholders – employees, customers, investors, strategic partners, the media – know what to think of this Brand? How are they supposed to figure out what the Brand is from one day to the next?

That's when it hit me. How the customer views the Brand is in fact what the Brand is. Nothing else matters. The company's execs and its marketing department, busily preparing their next brochure or ad campaign, might think they know what the Brand is, but all they really know is what they *want* the Brand to be at that moment. It is stakeholders, each and every one of them, who get to decide what the Brand is.

In other words, A Brand is what people think of you™.

Instinct

Every organization, whether business or not-for-profit, begins with an entrepreneur's vision to fulfill an unmet need. Somewhere along the line, I noticed that entrepreneurs, in contrast to managers trained at business schools, seemed to instinctively understand that their Brand was what people thought of them. They "just knew" that their Brand wasn't just their logo or their advertising. They grasped that their Brand was the sum of every experience ever had, by anyone, with their organization, their product or their service.

The name of our firm, Instinct, embraces the entrepreneur's instinctive understanding of Brand. As they launch their enterprises, entrepreneurs can easily articulate the key elements of their Brand, especially their core purpose, vision, mission, values and position. They might not even think of these foundational elements in terms of "Brand" – they might not even have a label for any of these thoughts – but they focus tightly and relentlessly on them and ensure they are delivered to customers with ruthless consistency. Because they understand that failure to do so means the end of their entrepreneurial dream.

The Brand Foundation

In a bid to protect client Brands from the whims of old friends and new friends, we at Instinct have adopted the entrepreneur's instinctive flair for Branding – by articulating the key Brand elements in a Brand Foundation. The Foundation is created to survive the marketing manager, executive or CEO who replaces you and yes, your own boredom or impatience. Its seven elements, discussed in detail in Chapters 4 and 6, are meant to crystallize the substance and spirit of the entrepreneur's view of his Brand and what it promises. So every employee can deliver on it, with the same instinctive ease as the entrepreneur, in every interaction.

Managers

As a humble former art school student, one of my early and erroneous assumptions was that the highly-paid, business school-trained executives at client organizations knew, by virtue of their education and job position, what a Brand really was. These were the men and women who were not entrepreneurs, but people who'd joined existing firms – folks who hadn't had to figure it all out for themselves and create something from nothing.

But eventually I realized that these professional managers thought a lot like the ad agencies did. They thought the Brand was basically the logo and the advertising. I would tell these managers that adopting proper Brand discipline could grow their organization to new heights. But here's a question

I've received, from a top executive no less, that epitomizes the level of mis-understanding still out there: "Branding? How the hell is a new logo going to turn around our company?"

Don't get me wrong: I like professional managers. Some of my best friends are professional managers. It's not their fault that they've always equated the Brand with the logo and the advertising. They think this way because the business schools they went to, no matter how highly regarded, only talked about Brand in marketing class. Because they only learned about Brand in marketing class, they relegate Brand management to their market-ing department when they become CEOs, and then they don't especially worry about it from that point onward.

CEOs

They don't realize that because a Brand is what people think of you, it's everything. It's every touchpoint that anyone ever has with your business. And when the Brand is this important, it can't be delegated away, but must be owned by the CEO – the only person in the organization with the clout to make sure that employees are delivering the Brand at each and every point of contact.

Branding: Not Just B2C

It's important for you to know that I'm not just talking about mass-market, business-to-consumer Brands like Subway or Maytag. Throughout this book I refer to such Brands often; because they are so widely known, they make for the most effective examples. But please keep in mind that the Brand dis-cipline I'm talking about applies equally to business-to-business, not-for-profit and government organizations. To every kind of organization there is.

If you apply the principles of this book to your organization, you'll see that they work.

This Book – Why Again?

The core purpose of my firm is this:
To advance the sustainability of North American organizations, reinforcing our free enterprise system and ensuring our continued prosperity as a society.

You might find this rather audacious. But I founded this firm because the

*It's what people think of you™

great majority of CEOs on this continent fundamentally misunderstand what Brand is all about, and I'm passionate about straightening them out. This updated book is an important part of that. I wrote the first edition as my last word on the topic, and to my surprise, there was a big appetite for it. *Brand: It Ain't the Logo** has been on the bestseller list of the *Globe and Mail*, Canada's newspaper of record, on and off for almost five years. I even turned down an offer to translate the book for publication in East Asia. The Asian economies have plenty of advantages over North America, so in keeping with my core purpose, I won't go out of my way to help them figure out Branding – because it is the only advantage we have left over them.

In the first edition of this book, I said that "leveraging this advantage is now more important than ever, because of three serious and growing threats to our prosperity." This time around, the situation is even more ominous.

I founded this firm because the great majority of CEOs on this continent fundamentally misunderstand what Brand is all about.

Threat #1: The Decline of Manufacturing

First is the deterioration of our manufacturing base, as epitomized by the depressing decline of the former "Big Three" U.S. automakers. Remember the hundreds of thousands of jobs lost at Ford, Chrysler and GM and the billions in taxpayer money spent bailing out the latter two. The weak Brand discipline of these companies had everything to do with their abysmal showing.

Ask just about anyone and they can easily tell you what differentiates BMW: "performance." Volvo: "safety." Ask those same people what Ford stands for and most of them will have no response at all. Of those with an answer, most will say something like "Found on Road Dead" or "Fix Or Repair Daily," and a small minority might say something like "tough" to describe Ford trucks. But most are at a complete loss for a word.

In 2006, CEO Bill Ford announced plant closings, layoffs of up to 25% of his company's workforce, and the need to build less expensive cars that people want. That same week, BMW announced record sales and profits on their premium-priced vehicles. Ford was so short on cash and Brand smarts that it chose not to invest in its Volvo Brand – owner of one of the world's strongest Brand positions – and ultimately sold it to Geely Automobile of China.

It's true that post-bailout, the Detroit automakers have made progress. I suggest in Chapter 7, for example, that Ford has had some success at reestablishing America's love affair with the car. But let's face it – led by carmakers like Toyota and BMW, foreign car Brands have differentiated themselves so clearly and consistently that since 2007, the former Big Three have sold less than 50% of cars purchased in the United States.

A lot of foreign carmakers seriously understand Brand. We'd better start understanding it too – to keep alive our automotive industry and wider manufacturing base, and also to prevent what is still unthinkable to almost every North American: the dominance of high-quality Chinese Brands.

Chinese Changes

You might think the previous sentence is a misprint, because many of us still think that all products made in China are crap. But we would be incorrect. For starters, the reason there are so many low-quality Chinese products is because we've been asking for them. For decades, Western wholesalers and retailers have been fattening their margins by demanding lower and lower prices from the Chinese manufacturers they've outsourced to – so the Chinese have simply been doing the rational thing and squeezing their quality.

Those same wholesalers and retailers have been hammering the Chinese to expand their production capacity while increasing their quality, on the promise of giving them more future business. So the Chinese have built thousands of factories sophisticated enough to make any American or Canadian manufacturer green with envy. In many of those sophisticated plants are being made some of the most prestigious Branded products in the world – including Reebok hockey and lacrosse equipment; Apple iPads, iPods and iPhones; Puma shoes; Sketchers shoes; Dell computers and Bose noise-cancelling headphones, to name just a few.

But because of the severe U.S. recession that started in 2008, much of the promised business didn't arrive.

*It's what people think of you™

And so we have a situation in which many of the shiny Chinese factories are sitting idle, and in which Chinese businesspeople are tired of Americans and Canadians getting more margin on the back of their lower and lower production costs. The net effect is that many Chinese have simply decided they're going to make their very own high-quality Brands and keep the margin for themselves.

Li-Ning

Li-Ning is one of those Brands. You've probably never heard of them – but stick around. Their stated Brand vision is *To be a world-leading brand in the sporting goods industry*. People in the know, however, know their real goal is to surpass Nike as the world's pre-eminent sportswear Brand. Can they actually achieve something so far-fetched?

They certainly intend to try. They opened a headquarters in the United States, a 15-minute drive from Nike corporate headquarters in Oregon. Then they headhunted a bunch of Nike's people and hired an American design firm that worked for Nike in the past. And they are getting some prominent endorsement deals with NBA players and other athletes.

Many Chinese have decided to make their own high-quality Brands and keep the margins for themselves.

Li-Ning not only wants to sell products in North America, they are already cutting into our share of the market in China itself. The Chinese have a voracious appetite for high-end Brands and regard them as prized symbols of status. Consider this: the Chinese government recently introduced a 25% import tax on Porsches entering the country for sale. When consumers heard about outrageously high Porsche prices, they went out and bought them in droves, and Porsche had its best year ever in China.

China: Not Just for Communists Anymore

Too many North Americans will still scoff that the Chinese come from a Communist system with only a short history of anything resembling capitalism.

19

And that therefore they lack the business education, money and entrepreneurial instincts to create competitive Brands of their own.

This point of view becomes more naïve all the time. China has an extremely wealthy upper class and oligarchy that has long been sending their kids to Europe and North America to figure out our methods. Nearly 150,000 Chinese students are enrolling in American universities every year. Of all foreign visa students at post-secondary institutions in Ontario, Canada's largest province, almost 30% are from China.

When they get home, they have a lot of people to sell to. China has a middle class larger than the entire population of the United States. By 2020, China is expected to be the largest consumer market in the world. By 2025, their middle class will reach 800 million people – well over double the entire projected American and Canadian populations.

Time to Wake Up

 Niall Ferguson is a high-profile professor of history at Harvard and the author of bestsellers including *The Ascent of Money: A Financial History of the World*. In a notable TED presentation, he spoke about what he calls "the great re-convergence." He was referring to how the East is rapidly closing its massive income gap with the West. He put it ominously:

> It's the biggest story of your lifetime. Because it's on your watch that this is happening. It's our generation that is witnessing the end of Western predominance. The average American used to be more than 20 times richer than the average Chinese. Now it's just five times, and soon it will be 2.5 times.

He also points out that the East is already leading us not in making crummy products, but in patents awarded – leading to the startling conclusion that they're leading us in innovation, which in the first book I said was still a North American advantage.

Here's the bottom line: a country with practically a billion and a half people – 20% of the world's total population – has figured out innovation and is starting to figure out Branding. This is why we must embrace Brand for what it really is. This is why it's imperative that we stop underestimating the Chinese and the East as a whole. The prosperity of our communities and our entire way of life depends upon the success of our emerging and big Brands. They are too important to fail.

Threat #2: The Labor Market Crisis

For the relatively few organizations with an accurate understanding of Brand, a very promising area of opportunity appears in the face of another threat we are only starting to wake up to: the labor shortage in many regions across the continent.

With over 70 million North American Baby Boomers scheduled to retire by 2020 and only 30 million workers to replace them, it's only going to get tougher to find the best employees, and then to keep them. If you think 2020 is too far away to worry about, keep in mind that even the very best organizations turn over 100% of their staff every 10 years, and super-strong Brands like Walmart and Starbucks have annual turnover rates approaching 100% at some locations.

Very few employers do a good job of communicating why Millennials – or anyone else – should work for them.

To boot, today's young workers – referred to as Generation Y or as Millennials – have different attitudes about work than the Boomers and Gen-Xers before them. In broad strokes, Boomers live to work and Gen-Xers work to live. Millennials, on the other hand, want to do work that aligns with their values and sense of purpose in life.

Very few employers today do a good job of communicating their core purpose, vision or values to potential customers, much less potential employees. If they hope to attract and retain Millennials, they must do a much better job of telling their story: of conveying why they exist, where they are going, what they stand for, and how a young person can be fulfilled by joining them.

Amid the worsening market for labor, a strong, clearly communicated Brand – embodied in a Brand Foundation and lived faithfully each day – helps potential employees (regardless of age) buy into and stick with your organization in a way that money alone simply cannot.

Threat #3: Hyper-messaging

The third threat we face is that of hyper-messaging – the overwhelming number of commercial messages that bombard us each day. Because of the increasing number of ways in which we receive media – and ironically, because of the ever-greater number of tools we have to block out commercial appeals – word of mouth is a more powerful weapon than ever for breaking through to stakeholders. As you'll see in Chapter 3, social media puts word of mouth on steroids and brings its own set of risks and opportunities.

Our entire way of life depends on the success of our Brands.

Branding Has Rules

Let's say that your favorite number is four. While sitting down with your accountant to review the financials in your business plan, would you ask that all the threes be changed to fours, just because you like them better?

When you're a Brand Coach, this type of thing is a regular request. It reflects the lack of awareness that Branding is a rule-based discipline like finance or accounting. So it's our job at Instinct to relate this maxim to clients: Branding is not a matter of personal taste. In the pages that follow, you'll see that each and every example of good Brand discipline is related to a maxim like this one, and in particular, these unbreakable tools and rules of Branding:

The Three Tools

1. **Be remark-able**
   - Because to break through the noise and reach your target market – and to avoid online wrath or irrelevance – your only option is to have a Brand worth talking about.

2. **Own a position**
   - Because to stand out in an overcommunicated world, you've got to establish and own a unique, honest, meaningful and clear difference.

3. **Deliver great experiences**
   - Because every stakeholder interaction either adds to or detracts from your Brand, you've got to deliver at every touchpoint.

The Three Rules

1. **Consistency**
   - Because constantly changing your messaging means that stakeholders won't be able to figure out who you are – making it impossible for you to get and keep their loyalty.

2. **Management**
   - Because if the CEO doesn't become the CBO (the Chief Brand Officer) and assume ultimate responsibility for ingraining a Brand Foundation into the organizational culture, employees won't deliver on it in every stakeholder interaction.

3. **Time**
   - Because if you want to earn and keep stakeholder mindshare over the long term, Branding must be understood as a process, not as an overnight event. So start now!

Brand: It ain't the logo*

*It's what people think of you™

[2] What "Brand" Really Means

Properly understood, the Brand has exciting potential to be the operating principle for everything your organization ever does.

"That was easy."

Staples

Let me tell you a story about a potential client that got away.

I was once approached by the CEO of a company whose products are in very wide distribution, but have very little Brand recognition. These products have approximately 40% market share in North America and are distributed through retailers like Costco, Walmart and Target. They can be found in homes and cottages everywhere, maybe including yours. Although you might really like this product and use it all the time, I'm guessing that its Brand is invisible to you. I'm willing to bet that unless you happen to be holding this product in your hands and scouring it for labels, you can't tell me what Brand it is.

So I met with the CEO on a few occasions to discuss how our firm might turn his product into a high recognition consumer Brand and give his sales a big push. Because Instinct defines a Brand as "what people think of you," I recommended to the CEO that our first step be to determine what people thought of his Brand by doing what we call a ThinkAudit™. A ThinkAudit is a concise survey of key Brand stakeholders including current and potential employees, customers and strategic partners.

Do People Think What You *Want* Them to Think?

Once we determined the differences between what we wanted people to think about the Brand and what they *actually* thought at that moment, we'd know how to move forward.

For example, the CEO and his leadership team viewed the position of their Brand as "classic." But did customers see it that way? If they didn't, we could determine the steps required to move customer thinking in that direction. And even if customers already perceived the "classic" position, was it the best strategic choice for the product, given the Brand positions of competitors? These are the kinds of crucial issues the ThinkAudit brings to light.

I didn't get the job. But I did get a very considerate email from the CEO, who kindly related that his decision was very tough to make. He was good enough to explain why he awarded the job to the other firm competing for his business.

He liked their logos better.

Brand: It Ain't the Logo

At the request of this potential client, I had submitted artwork of some logo designs I had directed over the years. The CEO and his team preferred the logos submitted by the other firm. He felt that the other firm would therefore hold greater respect in the eyes of his team.

I take full responsibility for failing to get through to this CEO who still thinks that a Brand is basically a logo. I take responsibility for not winning that client because folks, a Brand is most definitely not just a logo, or advertising, or a website, even though the majority of business leaders in North America think it is.

People are free to think whatever they want about you.

Your Brand Isn't Your Brand

A Brand is the sum total impression and memory of every remarkable, every so-so and every negative experience with any and all touchpoints of an organization. A Brand is the personality of an organization, product or service and is judged and assessed a value by everyone it touches, whether inside the organization (your employees) or outside (your customers, industry partners, strategic partners, shareholders and other stakeholders). These perceptions of value may, or may not, be what you want them to be. Which suggests a fact that may surprise you: your Brand isn't really yours. You don't own it – all the people thinking about you do.

Sure, you have legal ownership of your products and services, your business cards, your letterhead and yes, your logo – all the things you've thoughtfully produced with the goal of creating a certain impression in the minds of your stakeholders. But all the people out there own your Brand in the sense that, despite your very best efforts to craft a certain position for your Brand, people are free to think whatever they want about you.

The Only Synonym for "Brand" is "Culture"

In organizations that understand Brand, it drives every goal, informs every decision and shapes every message. These organizations establish a Brand Foundation describing precisely who they are, what they do, what they stand for and how they act. In other words, they define their culture. Which is why we say that the only synonym for "Brand" is "culture."

Then they have the discipline to "live" that culture by referring to their Brand Foundation each and every day. When a Brand Foundation is driving decisions, every contact with internal stakeholders nurtures the culture, and with external stakeholders, what you want them to think.

A clear, consistently articulated Brand is much more than marketing. It holds the principles around which your entire business is organized. Take Staples, the office supplies store, for example. When people think about Staples, chances are they think of the "Easy Button." That's because Staples has organized every aspect of their operation around the single, simple concept of making it easy for their customers to do business with them.

In 2001, Staples' revenue and profitability were a distant second to Office Depot in North America. Then they discovered that their most profitable customers weren't the masses they'd been pursuing with a low-price, big-box strategy, but harried small business owners with a narrow set of needs. People willing to sacrifice rock-bottom prices in favor of a quick, painless shopping experience. An easy shopping experience.

So Staples ditched their ceiling-scraping shelves and dizzying array of products –  because their market research told them that business owners don't have time to climb up product displays and they don't need 50 pens to choose from. Staples made it easy to shop on their website and ensured free, next-day delivery on orders of $50 or more. In-store, Staples staff are quick to offer help and ask, "Did you find everything you were looking for today?"

In the six years after Staples focused their Brand around "easy," revenue jumped from $11 billion to $18 billion. Profit skyrocketed 1000%, from $100 million to $1 billion – double the rise of Office Depot's profit over the same period. And Staples' stock price more than tripled.

Brand Potential

The way that Staples rallies its business around "easy" illustrates the potential of the Brand to be used as the operating principle for everything your organization ever does. In the arena of human resources management, for example, Staples hires only those people that can deliver on the promise of "easy" in everything they do. Making shelves more accessible to customers is a key merchandising decision. Carrying fewer pens and other products is an inventory management decision that has far-reaching implications for operations and cash flow. Not necessarily offering the lowest prices has a positive effect on profitability. The Easy Button has been a fantastically successful core idea around which to organize Staples' advertising and PR programs. And on it goes.

Branding: Not Just B2C

If you're a business-to-business firm, a not-for-profit or a part of government, right now you might be thinking that the example of Staples – a multibillion-dollar consumer Brand – doesn't apply to you.

Wrong.

More than half of Instinct clients are B2B, not-for-profit and government. It doesn't matter what your organization does: you can take a page from Staples and organize around the Brand. It may not be easy – but it will be worth it.

Brand: It ain't the logo*

*It's what people think of you™

[3] Be Remark-able

Brand-Building Tool #1

To break through the noise
and reach your target market
– and to avoid online wrath or
irrelevance – your only option
is to have a Brand worth
talking about.

"Advertising is the price you pay for having
an unremarkable product."

Jeff Bezos
CEO
Amazon.com

Years ago, I had the privilege of working with the smart folks who produced and marketed Cepacol, the mouthwash product. At the time, the market leader was Scope, which had the multimillion-dollar Procter & Gamble marketing machine behind it.

Cepacol, on the other hand, had Dow Chemical as its parent company. The industrial-strength boys at Dow were tight-fisted with their marketing money – so we had to be resourceful. What group, we wondered, could we get to flaunt its use of the product and, by association, make a powerful recommendation for the Brand?

We zeroed in on dental schools and made the product available for use by budding dentists who – no surprise – use more mouthwash than anybody. When these dentists graduated and continued to use the Brand their school had supplied, patients took note and did the same. Result: 26% market share and a highly profitable business.

Think Remark-able

My Cepacol experience got me thinking about the power of word-of-mouth – even though Cepacol was, frankly, not a remark-able product. I break up the word "remarkable" to emphasize its double meaning. When we use the word in everyday speech, we usually intend it to mean that something is interesting or noteworthy. We don't typically mean to convey the literal definition of "remarkable," which is that something is worth remarking about. So when I say remark-able, I'm referring to Brands so great that people just have to tell someone else about them. They're Brands so fantastic that they don't need advertising to catch on.

In a crazy, overcommunicated world, remark-ability is absolutely vital to building strong Brands. Our global economy has created a hyper-choice of goods, services and associated options in every category. In the early 1990s, for example, the average neighborhood grocery store stocked 11,000 individual items or SKUs (stock keeping units). In 2012, the average is 39,000 – and there are grocery superstores with more than 60,000. That's at least a threefold increase in choice, for an activity we have much less time to do.

With hyper-choice comes hyper-messaging, as marketers from Mumbai to Manhattan try to turn us into customers. Either as consumers or business-to-business buyers, we are hit with more than 3,500 commercial messages each and every day. It starts with ad jingles on the clock radio and moves

*It's what people think of you™

to the breakfast table with messages on the cereal box, newspapers and yesterday's mail. It continues en route to work – on subway platforms and inside buses, on billboards, trash cans, store windows and elevators. At the office it awaits on email, direct mail, trade advertising and sales calls both in person and over the phone. It doesn't break for lunch – appearing in food courts and along a lunchtime stroll or quick shopping expedition. Then there's a full repeat of the morning barrage on the trip home, followed by more mail, flyers and catalogues. And as you "relax" in front of the television, there are 23 minutes of commercials every hour – not to mention the emails you're answering on your laptop and the apps you're fiddling with on your smartphone.

Brands: Tools of Self-Defense

It's exactly this barrage that makes Brands, today, more important than ever before – because we use them as tools of self-defense. We defend ourselves from the advertising noise – in order to calm down and simplify our lives – by adopting Brands we know as "ours." Starbucks is one of "my" Brands, for example, and perhaps Gillette, or Coca-Cola, is one of "yours." We use our Brands as coping mechanisms because we can't possibly absorb the entire commercial barrage. If we're confronted with a message from one of our Brands, we might just pay attention to it. When I'm sorting through the junk mail I receive at home, for example, it's likely that I'll stop for a brief moment to consider a direct mailer from Lexus, because that's the car I drive. And if there's another car manufacturer sending me mail? They can forget about it.

Traditional Advertising Doesn't Work Anymore

Advertising these days costs a fortune, and for what? People tune it out anyway. We watch pay-per-view movies instead of network TV. We use call display to avoid facing the next hapless telemarketer. We skip radio commercials by using iPods, employ popup blockers while surfing the Net, and thank goodness for our spam filters.

It used to be easy for advertisers to reach us. In the 1960s and 70s, Walter Cronkite, legendary anchorman of the CBS Evening News, had 50 million view-

ers. The population of the United States at the time was in the area of 190 million, so Cronkite, "the most trusted man in America," spoke directly to almost 25% of Americans every night. And so did the companies that booked advertising with the CBS Evening News.

Contrast that with 2011. NBC, ABC, CBS, CNN and MSNBC had a combined 25 million viewers. That's just half of what Cronkite commanded all by his lonesome. And the population of the United States in 2011 was 313 million, so all six of these news organizations – and the companies that booked advertising with them – were reaching a combined total of just 8% of the American public.

Social Media

With the quick rise of YouTube and its genre, the economics of the entire television industry are undergoing a violent shake-up. Consumers have skipped TV ads for years, but now they're skipping TV itself. We are instead heading en masse to the Internet and its channels of social media. Simply put, there's never been a better time to have a great Brand, or a worse time to have one that stinks. Consumers have always shared their opinions with friends and even strangers. But social media is word of mouth on steroids. Lots of steroids.

Twitter has hundreds of millions of tweets per day. Facebook has millions of comments made and links shared every few minutes. Embedded in this buzz are legions of brutally frank opinions on products and services. When our (or a friend's) Facebook status says "Annoyed. Waiting in line at ____ bank for 30 minutes!" or "Love my new iPhone," followers take notice and adjust their view of Brands accordingly. Likewise for the more structured opinion-sharing channels: who among us hasn't checked Trip Advisor before taking a vacation, or Amazon reviews before buying that perfect gift?

Juicy Reviews

One of our Brand Coaches was shopping at Crate and Barrel for a juicer to give as a present. She admits having absolutely no clue about what features to look for, what the top Brands were or what a reasonable price should be.

Did she consult a salesperson? Of course not. She Googled the two products in front of her and the first search results were from Amazon. The first juicer had a whopping 411 customer reviews, 360 of them 5-star. The second juicer didn't even come close, and the shopping trip was over.

The Long Tail

With more than two billion people and counting on the Internet, remarkability is now your only option. Yet ironically, social media is not just about the masses – about earning their praise and avoiding their wrath. It's also about the exact opposite – about reaching what Chris Anderson calls "the long tail."

In his book of the same name, Anderson argues that our culture and economy is increasingly shifting away from focusing on a relatively small number of mainstream products and markets at the head of the demand curve, and toward a huge number of niches in the tail. Social media enables us to capitalize on the long tail by targeting our products and services to people who share extraordinarily narrow niches of interest. These people access their interests online, through search engines like Google and countless blogs and other social media elements such as Twitter and Facebook.

Like people who really love scissors. Yes, scissors. Fiskars is a scissor company that is more than 360 years old and has thousands of avid Facebook followers. Fiskars realized that scrapbookers were extremely passionate about their hobby – so they focused their business around this niche group. They used social media to create an inspiring conversation – not about Fiskar products, but about the community of scrapbooking artists and what they've been able to create.

Fiskars has acted upon hundreds of innovations suggested by their followers, or "Fiskateers." The Fiskateers have rewarded the company by raising sales 300% since its online presence was established.

For Branders, the Fiskars story should be wonderfully inspirational. As we will see in the next chapter, adopting a clear and unique Brand position (defined as *How we make a difference*) is a fundamental component of good Brand discipline. Yet it's very scary, because adopting a single position means forgoing all others. So most Brands water down their point of difference in an effort to avoid alienating anyone. The result, instead, is a Brand that doesn't deeply resonate with anyone.

The Fiskars example tells us that it's safer than ever to define a narrow Brand position, because social media allows us to leverage remark-ability into connecting with lots of people who share a narrow niche.

Purple Cow

Remark-ability is the central theme of *Purple Cow*, Seth Godin's best-selling marketing book[1]. If you're driving through the country and see a brown cow, and then a white cow, or even a white cow with black spots, chances are they won't even register in your conscious mind. Who hasn't seen your run-of-the-mill bovine? They're not worth telling anyone about.

But then you see a cow that's purple. You'd better believe you're going to be stopping the car to get a better look. You'll be sure to snap a few photos and Tweet them or post them to Facebook. And when you get over your fascination with the colorful beast, you're going to tell everyone you know, and even those you don't, about your experience.

Social media makes it safer than ever to define a narrow Brand position.

What's Your Purple Cow?

Godin's metaphor asks us the question: "So: what's your purple cow?" And if your answer is "We don't have one," or, "Sure, we have one" but it's nothing more than a typical Holstein, Godin strongly suggests (and I wholeheartedly agree) that you get back to the drawing board and paint that cow purple.

Going the Distance

Most Brands would readily admit that word of mouth is infinitely less expensive than advertising. Yet they continue to advertise heavily because they simply don't know how to be remark-able. What they need to do is seize upon the reality that a Brand is what people think of you. And that Brand equity is the *value* of what people think of you. And that developing remark-ability is the starting point of building that value.

The Running Room, North America's largest specialty running retailer, does it by delivering an experience so great, customers just have to tell someone. This company does a lot more than sell sneakers: they create an integrated Brand experience that begins with all staff being runners themselves. They therefore understand your challenges and needs as a customer – comprehension that's the basis of superior service delivery. And superior products, including a Running Room Brand of premium-quality footwear, apparel and accessories.

These same staff members broaden the Brand experience by hosting running groups and clinics to help you train for a marathon or other race (many of which the Running Room sponsors), or even learn how to run in the first place. The Running Room community is further intensified through online forums, where customers are very active at sharing info on everything from training techniques to carpooling.

It all adds up to a Brand that isn't just differentiated, but that's creating a unique and meaningful difference in a very competitive industry. To a Brand that gets customers talking.

Early Adopters

When you have a remark-able product, you can rely on your early adopters in place of traditional, expensive advertising methods – because you don't need those traditional, expensive advertising methods any more. You still, however, need creativity and resourcefulness. iPod, Starbucks, Lululemon, 1-800-GOT-JUNK? ...remark-able products and services all, that for the most part were introduced without a great deal of traditional advertising.

Apple has produced some beautiful and brilliant ads for its iPod franchise, but initially it was just the brilliance of the product, those white cords and the contented grins of the cool user group that generated interest and sales.

The Starbucks phenomenon has grown across North America and around the world on the strength of its remark-ability. Little mass advertising has ever been used to build the Brand. Rather, people have adopted the Brand for themselves by wandering in to investigate what a friend told them was a cool coffee experience.

The Manifesto

Created in 1998 by Chip Wilson, Lululemon designs, produces and sells yoga-inspired athletic wear through its own stores across North America, Australia, New Zealand and China. This Brand was built on the simple and indisputable notion that women will buy clothing that makes their bodies look absolutely fantastic. Then add the Lululemon Manifesto, which offers mantras like "Colas are NOT a substitute for water. Colas are just another cheap drug made to look great by advertising."

Lighthearted statements like "Dance, sing, floss and travel" accompany the Coke diatribe to portray a worldview that's one part Deepak Chopra, one part Michael Moore. The colorful, beautiful products are well thought out, well made and sold by genuinely nice people. The entire experience is a Brand broadcast that allows the perfect consumer to self-identify, connect with the culture, buy and start telling the Lululemon story to others.

Lululemon's remark-ability has almost completely removed the need for them to advertise. Here are some remark-ably astonishing facts for you to consider: a full-page ad in a major national newspaper costs in the area of $30,000; in 2006, when Lululemon was capitalized at $191 million, the company spent a total of just *$37,000 on advertising*; the next year, Chip sold 48% of the firm, which went public and grew by a factor of 41 – to $7.74 billion – over the next four years.

Wow.

The Emotional Side of Junk

1-800-GOT-JUNK?, billed as the world's largest junk removal service, got that way by, remark-ably, positioning junk removal as an issue of emotional health for household-running women. JUNK? zeroed in on the great feeling of organization and order these ladies get from cleaning out their nasty basement or embarrassing backyard.

JUNK?'s remark-able position allowed them to set and surpass some very lofty goals. They made it an objective to appear on *Oprah*, a direct channel to millions of North American women, in their first two years of business. They did it inside of one. Next was an appearance on the *Dr. Phil* show. On both occasions the theme of discussion was how cleaning up your living space is part of setting your life in order.

*It's what people think of you™

JUNK?'s affiliation with *Hoarders*, the weekly A&E reality show, is an especially powerful demonstration of how emotional junk removal can be. *Hoarders* features people with a very serious psychological issue – they can't throw anything away. An episode shot in Manhattan is typical: a man has packed so much stuff into his 4th-floor apartment, he has to sleep on a bench in the street. The only way he can get in is by climbing the fire escape and then tunneling through the junk.

After the hoarder receives counseling from a trained psychologist, JUNK? arrives in dramatic style. Four of its sparkling white-and-blue trucks appear, and their impeccably-dressed crews of polite, considerate young gentlemen get to work and clean the place out.

From mayhem to order in 60 minutes, it's remark-able Brand building – every week in prime time.

What are You Doing to be Remark-able?

With today's global markets and unlimited availability of goods and services, the world quickly discards unremark-able Brands. So go right back to the beginning. Stare your product or service square in the face. Does it have remark-ability? Be brutally honest with yourself. Ask others for their brutally honest opinions. Because just as today's connected consumers can spread the word about a great product, they can – and will – spread the word about a dud even faster.

When developing your remark-able product, use success stories like iPod and Lululemon as your guide. Make it easy for a wave of referrals to spread by maximizing the disciplines these companies have followed: have a memorable name, an easy-to-use website and an experience for your customers to rave about. And it never hurts to have a beautifully-designed product that people proudly display or wear.

But getting people to relate your Brand story to others is only part of the equation. That story must also be easy to tell.

Brand: It ain't the logo*

*It's what people think of you™

[4] Own a Position

Brand-Building Tool #2

To stand out in our overcommunicated world, you've got to establish and own a unique, honest, meaningful and clear position.

"In celebration of the fact that Pizza Hut will now deliver restaurant-quality pasta across the nation, the famed franchise is officially changing its name to 'Pasta Hut' (on a temporary basis)."

Pizza Hut
Press release

If you walk into your local grocery store and are confronted with 20 shelf feet of unknown ketchups, buying a bottle suddenly gets complicated. Multiply that 20 feet of shelf space by all the items on your list, and food shopping gets difficult beyond imagination. But because we have our favorite Brands, the ones we've come to know and trust and have filed away in the hard drives of our minds, we can simply grab our Brand and get on with living.

The ketchup aisle is a great example of Brands as tools of self-defense because one Brand completely dominates the category – Heinz. Their packaging is recognizable to the extent that customers might not even read the name on it before grabbing the bottle off the shelf. To prove this ironic point – that we know the Brand so well we don't consciously register what it looks like – I sometimes ask clients to describe three things on the Heinz label. They almost never can – because Heinz owns the "best tasting ketchup" position so completely, it is imprinted on our subconscious.

Creating a Unique Position

The Brand Foundation is discussed in Chapter 6. Yet one element, the position (*How we make a difference*) is so important to Branding success, it gets this chapter all to itself.

The position is your unique offering in the marketplace that separates you from competitors. It is a meaningful difference that you authentically own.

To own stakeholder brainspace even approaching that of Heinz, you need to stake out a position that really matters – a position that people can really buy into. And while you might dream of making a customer out of every last living human being, a Brand must select a position – sometimes targeted to a very narrow market – that will differentiate it loudly and clearly from competitors.

Deliberate Alienation

Deliberately ruling out a whole bunch of customers takes guts. But think about what Abercrombie & Fitch has done. Surely you've seen their identity – in the form of *Abercrombie, Fitch, A & Fitch* and other combinations – on the preppy t-shirts, sweatshirts and hoodies worn by seemingly every other teen.

Abercrombie's grip on the high school psyche is a case study in profoundly strong positioning – based upon a very different retail experience. Stand in

*It's what people think of you™

the middle of a Tristan America, Mexx or French Connection UK at the mall, for example, and you'll be hard pressed to see much difference among them.

Not so with Fitch, where the experience begins 100 feet before you even see the store. That's where the first wafts of Abercrombie-Branded cologne, sprayed by staff on their mannequins every 30 minutes, hits the nostrils. Borrowing from the exclusivity-building techniques of swishy nightclubs, the store exterior turns retail merchandising on its head with forbidding wooden blinds that give no hint to the goods inside.

There, the nightclub motif continues: it's half-lit, with spotlights pointing out displays. It's loud: trendy rock necessitates yelling at anyone further than arm's length away. It's sexy: 8-foot-high black and white prints of half-naked college kids – impossibly thin, beautiful and upper crust – dominate the sightlines. You might even be greeted by one of the male models in the flesh – shirtless, ripped and selected from the Abercrombie staff.

Dare to be Very Different

The logic of positioning is that occupying a single spot means sacrificing all others. It's a scary proposition for many organizations, because they're afraid of losing customers at the fringes of their target market. So they dilute their Brand at the expense of resonating deeply with anyone.

That's what makes Abercrombie & Fitch so gutsy. Their Brand is so different, and so in-your-face, that it deliberately and instantly alienates the scores of people who don't like the exact experience on offer. The bargain for Fitch, and for any Brand that dares to be very different, is a cohort of customers deeply committed to precisely what's for sale.

Be Consistent

Once you own mindshare like A&F, you've got to work hard to keep it – by being ruthlessly consistent. When a Brand changes what it says, how it looks or how it behaves, current and potential customers start to wonder if the offering is the same. That's because a consistent, strong Brand forms a shortcut in the buyer's decision-making process. Consistent Brands own a certain mindshare, and when you mess with the Brand, that mindshare goes up for sale again. Whereas the consistent Brand is a shortcut allowing the consumer to exert near-zero brainpower on what to buy in a particular category, the changed Brand cues the mind to reopen its decision-making process to include other Brands all over again. The buying decision is no longer a no-brainer. All competitors have been reintroduced.

Hut for What?

A Brand is what people think of you. And if you don't know what your Brand is, no one else will either.

Pizza Hut is a case in point. With 13,000 restaurants in 100 countries, this Brand is the world's largest company in its category. Yet at times its messaging has been extremely inconsistent and confusing.

In 2009, it was reported that Pizza Hut had changed its name to simply "The Hut." A company spokesman "clarified" the situation, however, by saying that the Brand would not be changing its name, but rather: "the boxes and some store signs will say 'The Hut.' Others will retain the Pizza Hut name."

And with the launch of a new pasta offering came this press release: "In celebration of the fact that Pizza Hut will now deliver restaurant-quality pasta across the nation, the famed franchise is officially changing its name to 'Pasta Hut' (on a temporary basis)."

Huh??

To cap it all off, Pizza Hut introduced WingStreet Wings, a sub-Brand that further muddies the company's Brand position.

So exactly what is that position? Is Pizza Hut a pasta place, a pizza place, a wings joint, all three or none of the above? Good questions I suspect company leadership would be hard-pressed to answer. Pizza Hut might try mightily to be everything to everyone, but it can't. You can't either.

Quiznos' Position: Toast(ed)

Ditto for Quiznos. Only a handful of Brands have the strategic genius to stake out a position that is truly meaningful and memorable, along with the discipline to communicate it with relentless consistency. Quiznos used to be one of them.

Think Volvo and "safety." Think Subway and "healthy." These quick and easy, single-word associations are extremely rare. They are priceless corporate assets that give these smart Brands a huge advantage over the great majority of competitors whose points of difference are less clear.

Now, what comes to mind when you think of Quiznos? For most people, it's "toasted." It's a position Quiznos has steadily conveyed through positioning statements like *Toasted tastes better*. Their complete ownership of the toasted position even alarmed Subway – *which has twenty-five thousand more stores* – into installing toasting ovens.

But Quiznos turned its back on toasted by introducing a new positioning statement: *Love what you eat*. What meaningful Brand position does that reflect? That Quiznos offers great-tasting food? It's not exactly a unique approach in a category that's about indulging your appetite.

But wait, you might say: Subway's ovens forced Quiznos to change position. Nonsense. Most Brands have offerings similar to their competitors. Consider that Volvo is hardly the only automaker talking about safe cars – they've just had the discipline to live their safety position more consistently than anyone.

The House that Jared Built

Subway is in their second decade with Jared, the guy who lost 245 pounds eating subs and who exemplifies their "healthy" Brand position and *Eat Fresh* positioning statement. Subway had the brains to part ways with at least four ad agencies who, as ad agencies are hardwired to do, wanted to make their mark by doing something new. Except that on the coattails of Jared, Subway doubled its stores to more than 30,000 and its sales to over $8 billion. We can all learn something from their admirable commitment to consistency.

A Beautiful Mind(share)

Maybe they learned something from Volvo. If you show the Volvo logo to a room full of people and ask them for the first thing that comes to mind, I guarantee you someone will call out "safety." In fact, you could even show the word "safety" to a room full of people and ask them what Brand comes to mind, and I guarantee you someone will say "Volvo." It's a remark-able

*It's what people think of you™

thing to witness. This despite half-hearted support from Ford, Volvo's past owner.

How is Volvo still the undisputed owner of safety? Mainly through exceptional consistency. They defined their Brand position in 1927 with these words from their founders: "Safety is and must be the basic principle in all design work." The Brand's people have lived this position at every touchpoint and conveyed exceptionally consistent messaging over a great length of time.

Specifically, they invented many of the automobile safety advances of the past century, including the world's first laminated windshield (1944), rear-facing child seat (1964) and blind spot information system (2004). There is an area on their website called "How Volvo saved my life," in which Volvo owners are invited to recount a brush with serious injury or death while in their cars. It is said that in Sweden, Volvo's country of origin, the first three parties to arrive at the scene of a car accident are the police, ambulance and Volvo engineers – there to figure out what went wrong, and how they might prevent it with their next innovation.

Uncovering a point of difference that's truly meaningful to your target audience is no easy task.

Pick a Position that Matters

Of course, Volvo's choice of position has been a major contributor to the mindshare they own. Safety has always been highly relevant in the car market, and one expects it always will be. If Volvo had chosen in 1927 to stick two steering wheels in their cars and differentiate on that basis, things wouldn't have worked out quite so well.

Uncovering a point of difference that's truly meaningful to your target audience is no easy task. And so my great respect for the positioning statement of Dyson's vacuum cleaner line: *The vacuum cleaner that doesn't lose suction.* It's a promise that stands out from the competition. Like Zipcar's *Wheels when you want them* and Porter Airlines' *Flying refined*, it resonates because there's a problem to be solved and these guys have solved it.

Dyson's line of household fans? Not so much. They boast that their fans don't "buffet" the air ("buffet" defined as "to strike against or push repeatedly: The wind buffeted the house"). There are many problems in this world that require solving, but I venture to say that fans buffeting the air is not one of them. The question that Dyson and all Brands must ask is: "How do we describe our position, and does that position matter to stakeholders?"

Brand Capitalization

WestJet, who modelled their fleet management and customer service approach on Southwest Airlines, is a Brand that's leveraged a very meaningful position into some serious brainspace. WestJet demonstrates how capitalizing on a competitor's point of weakness can result in position ownership that is very difficult to contest.

Air Canada is WestJet's main competitor in Canada and has a brutal reputation for customer service. Realizing customer service to be Air Canada's Achilles heel, WestJet took direct aim with a Brand position of "caring."

For example, a well-known television spot shows a female flight attendant returning a cell phone to a startled businessman on a downtown street, days after his flight. Not only is she returning his phone, she has been fielding his calls – getting him "$50 above the asking price" on the Jet Ski he apparently had for sale. The ad ends with a question and answer: "Why do WestJetters care so much? Because we're also WestJet owners."

Again, marketing communications that don't represent reality will not sustain your purported position for long. Unique, ownable positions are based on a Brand's essential truths. In the case of WestJet, it seems we can safely assume that the reason its employees actually do deliver friendly, fun and thoughtful customer service is at least partly because they own shares in the company.

The persuasive power of telling an authentic, cohesive story cannot be understated. Consider this: WestJet has been so effective at communicating its story of caring that most Canadians have no idea the rest of the world holds their favorite punching bag in very high esteem. Air Canada has, in fact, received numerous international awards – including Best Airline in North America in a huge Skytrax survey of 17 million passengers worldwide.

*It's what people think of you™

Why hasn't Air Canada been able to shake their terrible reputation in their home and native land? Because WestJet seized a highly meaningful position, consistently provides great experiences and then talks about it. They've painted Air Canada into a corner.

Your Brand Competes with Everything

Underlining the need for consistency is the realization that you're not battling with competitors in just your industry. Your Brand has to fight its way through all of the hyper-messaging hitting your target market, whether it's related to your industry or not. The narrower your Brand position is, the tighter the target market is for your message – and the better your ability to reach that market, stake it out and by being consistent, eventually own it.

Be Different, Be Consistent

Articulate your precise point of difference with a meaningful Brand position. Embed it in an overall Brand Foundation (discussed in Chapter 6) and in everything you do. Then communicate it to stakeholders while always, always keeping in mind the number one rule of Branding: be consistent.

[5] A Brand's Worst (and Next Worst) Enemies

At this very moment, there are people conspiring against your Brand. They may be keen up-and-comers or some of your most trusted long-term associates. One thing is for certain: they must be stopped.

"We underestimated the deep emotional bond [consumers had with the brand packaging]."

Neil Campbell
President
Tropicana

It's easy to see why so many people make the mistake of equating marketing communications – including logos, advertising and other tools – with the Brand itself.

It's because we humans are visually dominant beings. We recognize a face before we remember that person's name. We think in pictures. We need to close our eyes to listen more closely. The power of this overriding human sense is the key reason that marketing communications are so often confused with being the Brand itself.

Your marketing communications are simply manifestations of what you want your Brand to be. People in your stakeholder groups – your employees, customers, strategic partners, investors, the media, everyone – have interpreted these manifestations, along with other information they've received about you, and have developed opinions on what you are. Which leads us back to the fact that a Brand is what people think of you.

If we want our stakeholders to see the Brand the way we want them to, we must first decide exactly who we are in terms of Brand Foundation elements. Then we must ensure that when using marketing communications, we convey these elements with relentless consistency. It is consistency – the number one rule of Branding – that cues, in the minds of customers, that a given message is from one of "their" Brands. In terms of marketing communications, these consistent cues include:

- Context – as in Apple making frequent use of billboards
- Tone and manner – we recognize an Apple billboard long before we're close enough to read it
- Core idea – Staples' Easy Button, Subway's Jared
- Sounds – the Intel riff
- And the strongest cue: visual identity, including color (orange for Home Depot) and graphics (the Nike swoosh)

Old Friends

The enemies of Brand consistency lurk everywhere. Worst are "old friends" – the people inside the organization who are so tired of their own messaging, they assume everyone else is too. Old friends will agree to any new Brand message ideas that come along, just to get away from their same old Brand position or incessant jingle. They're the people at Coca-Cola who are sick

*It's what people think of you™

and tired of giving (or receiving) another red t-shirt; the folks at Energizer who'd just as soon blow up that bunny as see him or hear his beating drums.

MasterCard

MasterCard has done a fine job of keeping the inevitable old friends in check. The Brand's "Priceless" advertising campaign was launched in 1997 ("There are some things money can't buy. For everything else there's MasterCard"). Created by McCann-Erickson, the Priceless ads have been seen in more than 100 countries and translated into 50-plus languages. The spots don't just enjoy incredibly high awareness; they've embedded MasterCard into the popular culture. Some people actually spend their time writing jokes and piecing together funny videos that build up to the "Priceless" punchline. Maybe you've received one in your email inbox, or visited YouTube.com – where a search for MasterCard spoofs yields hundreds of results.

MarineLand

MarineLand is another model of Brand consistency. It's a popular aquatic theme park on the Canadian side of Niagara Falls. Because of the cold climate, the park only operates from May to October each year. For many families, a visit to the park is an annual ritual.

For as many springs as anyone can recall, MarineLand has run television and radio ads with an unforgettable musical jingle. There's something special about it that lodges in your brain, but in a pleasant way that makes you want to hum it or sing it out loud. I have heard of a young mother whose baby instantly stopped fussing and crying whenever the ad came on TV.

If owning mindshare is tough enough with year-round contact, it's extremely difficult for seasonal Brands that disappear for months at a time. So wouldn't it seem sensible to exercise consistency in the use of advertising, as MarineLand has done to such great effect?

Of course – but it's tougher than you might think. Imagine telling someone in the Niagara Falls area that you work at MarineLand. You know what's coming next – some comment about the jingle. You might even be treated to a few off-key bars.

Truth is, you can't escape the darn thing. And you assume everybody's just as ready for a change as you are.

Wrong. Consumers are over burdened with new commercial messages. They're highly receptive to a friendly, familiar reminder – be it another red t-shirt, the Energizer Bunny, "Priceless," or the MarineLand jingle.

Rise of the Panic Brands?

Global economic turmoil has everyone scared. It could be that in the Branding world, old friends are responding to the crisis by birthing a new species: the Panic Brand.

Take Tropicana Pure Premium orange juice, for instance. For years, their carton has easily been the most recognizable on the shelf. Its bright graphics – of a big juicy orange with a straw stuck in it – clearly convey Tropicana's premium position and fundamental difference from the "from concentrate" competition. The orange and straw comprise a core idea that speaks volumes about the Brand's position in a way meaningful and compelling to the target audience.

And yet, in the United States, Tropicana actually took the graphics on its instantly recognizable carton and changed them to something utterly different and downright generic – something suggesting a product as far from premium as could be. Gone was the iconic orange with straw. Gone were legions of loyal customers, who couldn't find their favorite Brand anymore.

Oops.

In less than two months, sales dropped 20%. Tropicana was forced into the costly move of reverting to its old packaging. That cost, of course, on top of the *$35 million* CBS reported was spent changing the carton in the first place[2].

Image Recognition Software

What were they thinking? It could be that they've surrendered to the panic sweeping other iconic Brands. Much in the way that giants like Walmart and Kraft have changed their logos to appear (in their opinion) more consumer-friendly in frightening times, Tropicana might have thought that softening their categorically premium position would hold sales steady.

Old friends at Tropicana's parent, PepsiCo, don't realize that in our overcommunicated world, we're not reading ads and logos anymore. We're taking mental snapshots with the image recognition software in our brains. On that note, PepsiCo isn't limiting itself to changing just Tropicana. It was the parent's old friends who recently crashed my brain at the local gas station – by having no less than three different logos on display for regular Pepsi.

A Brand's Next Worst Enemies

If old friends are a Brand's worst enemies, who are the next worst? That's right: "new friends."

Together, old friends and new friends conspire to destroy consistency, your most powerful Brand-building weapon. They're an especially virulent problem as your firm grows. As more and more people make decisions that affect your organization and Brand, it becomes tougher to be consistent because the new blood in your organization – an unholy alliance of new staff and the outside creative suppliers they hire – is chomping at the bit to make their mark. Old friends – tired and bored as they are – are only too eager to act as accomplices.

New employees want to put their personal stamp on everything. They want to demonstrate their creativity, frequently by doing exactly what they did in their old job (they got hired on the strength of their past work, so why not keep doing it?). So they'll go about trying to impress by applying their vision to your products, business cards, flyers, radio commercials, recruiting materials, training videos, email formats, websites, reception area – everything.

Sleeman's Slippery Slope

New friends contributed mightily to the downward slide and sale of the once independently-owned Sleeman Breweries. In the 1980s, John Sleeman decided to revive the family brewery, founded by his great-great-grandfather but long dormant, and do what many thought was completely insane at the time: enter a Canadian market in which two players – Molson of Montreal and Labatt of Toronto – split nearly 100% market share.

Integrity.
Est. 1834

Sleeman's Brand was very different from the start. While the Goliaths were selling an array of indistinguishable beers by bouncing from one bikini-driven message to another, Sleeman stayed consistent. Radio spots featured John Sleeman himself talking about the family heritage and his beer's

*It's what people think of you™

premium quality. This laser-like focus earned Sleeman a crystal-clear position and customers happy to fork over premium prices compared to the majors. They steadily cut into the big boys' market share, grabbing in the area of 10%, a truly astounding figure given the utter dominance of Molson and Labatt to that point.

Bikini Beer

But then John got busy with his success and the demands of an initial public offering. At about the same time I noticed that the Brand position was changing – they were introducing scores of new Brands like Sleeman Clear, a watery product designed to cash in on the "low-carb" craze but fundamentally at odds with Sleeman's premium taste position. Even more surprising, instead of talking about heritage and quality, they were rolling out a bunch of clichéd ads chock-a-block with deck parties and bodacious babes.

I sent John an email to ask what was going on. He replied that his new marketing friends inside the business knew what they were doing, thank you very much. They were going with deck parties and babes because Sleeman's Branding came across as too "old" for the younger generation of beer drinkers they wanted to attract.

But wait: weren't the original drinkers of Sleeman products, when they were first introduced in the late 80s, young themselves? Yes they were. The heritage and quality appeals worked then and there's no reason to believe they wouldn't work again with another generation of young drinkers.

And guess who John's new friends were? The marketers formerly of Molson and Labatt. The same people who had turned their backs on the Brand potential of those legendary institutions and repositioned them so many times as to make them nearly meaningless – all while Sleeman drank millions of their market share.

John ultimately issued a profit warning and dropped his premium prices to compete head-to-head with the Brands selling beers for a buck. Not long after, Sleeman was sold to Sapporo Breweries of Japan, becoming (after Molson and Labatt) the third and final major Canadian brewery laid to rest in foreign hands.

Creatives

Ad agencies and their creatives like to think that new ideas are their reason for being, when in truth, new ideas are their fundamental problem.

In exchange for creating new – the exact opposite of consistent – creatives are rewarded with pay raises, bonuses, promotions and new job offers. They are celebrated and even worshipped – especially by the mutual appreciation society that is the advertising industry – for creating that which has never been seen. This is an industry that congratulates itself at a glitzy awards show in Cannes, for heaven's sake. And you'll never win an award for working with an old idea, even if it serves the Brand well.

"Fresh," not "New"

These creatives may or may not realize that coming up with something fresh is actually a lot harder than dreaming up something new. Being fresh requires that you always work in a single, unchanging context: what the Brand actually stands for. New, on the other hand, means the freedom to start over on a clean canvas every time.

These creatives may not realize that coming up with something fresh is a lot harder than dreaming up something new.

Rats!

I thought that 1-800-GOT-JUNK? would be one outfit capable of resisting the temptations of new creative friends. JUNK?'s female-targeted Branding reflects that more often than not, it's the woman of the household who makes decisions about cleaning up the place.

One day I received a call from the leadership of a JUNK? franchise, who wanted my opinion on an ad campaign a new agency was pitching them. The agency was proposing "funny" TV spots in which rats – yes, rats – were being thrown out of the organization's distinctively blue trucks onto suburban front lawns. The ad cuts to housewives screaming in horror at the rat invasion. The tagline for the campaign? *Call us before we send you rats.*

It was a campaign that threatened to take all the Brand equity earned from talk show appearances in front of tens of millions of North American women and throw it not on the lawn, but on the proverbial junk pile. It's a potent illustration of new friends' compulsion to always do something new. I thought to myself: thank goodness the JUNK? boys checked with me before rolling over for some creatives itching to make their mark.

But my relief was misplaced. The rats ad not only went ahead, but won an award at one of the ad industry's many festivals of self-congratulation – persuasive evidence that the new advertising diverts from what was a hugely effective Brand message. I could summarize the discipline of Brand consistency in the form of a question to the JUNK? people: "if it ain't broke, why 'fix' it?"

Toshiba

Years ago, Toshiba positioned their notebook computers as the tough ones that could take the bumps of everyday life and still be counted on to work. Chiat Day, the hot creative shop of the time, came up with a brilliant TV campaign called "I can't believe I checked my notebook!" The 30-second story featured a hapless business traveler who inadvertently checked his notebook at the airline counter and only realized it at 30,000 feet. After a fretful flight he is rewarded when his Toshiba notebook boots up following a tough trip through the baggage handling system.

So successful was the ad that Toshiba began to gain on IBM's market share. Toshiba management asked Chiat Day for the next ad in the series. But those hotshots refused to do a mere sequel. Toshiba fired them and hired my firm to create the sequel – "Follow that cab!" – in which our same hero chases down his notebook after placing it on the trunk of an airport taxi. The commercial leveraged the equity of the first ad and helped drive Toshiba to market share leadership.

So why wasn't there a third ad in the series, and a fourth? Why isn't the Toshiba campaign still running today? You guessed it – because old friends at Toshiba, to the detriment of their Brand, were evidently bored stiff by their own messaging.

Spend Less Time, Make More Money

One of the best things about proper Brand discipline is that it's one of the few business realms in which, if you want to succeed, you never have to do anything completely new. The surest path to lower expenses, higher revenue and increased Brand equity is to simply be consistent.

Ask anyone who's ever heard of Tim Hortons what promotional campaign they will run this year, and they will probably say "Roll up the Rim." It is an annual campaign – now more than 25 years old – anxiously awaited by millions in Canada and the northeastern United States.

How many years do you think it would take Tim Hortons to dream up an alternative campaign – one that could take the place of Roll up the Rim, one that could build as much or more Brand equity? At least 25, I'd say. And it would cost a whole lot of money to boot.

The lesson: keep your messaging consistent from period to period, year to year. Enjoy the enormous savings in man hours and production costs that come from avoiding 'constant, costly and unnecessary retoolings. Then enjoy the biggest bonus of all – more time to build Brand equity by focusing on the core issues of your business.

Remember this rule of thumb: just when people inside your organization are getting bored of your Brand message, your target market is just starting to notice it.

It's a truism that underscores how important it is to control your Brand's friends, old and new. Communicate to those folks who seem to be itching for a change that Brand consistency is good not just for the business, but for them. Tell them that the way to make a mark is not by changing the Brand message but by helping solidify  it. Challenge your creative suppliers to do fresh, not new. And say a polite goodbye to the ones trying to sell you change for its own sake.

You are Not Alone

In your fight against those who would change your Brand, you are not alone. At your disposal is an especially crucial weapon in the Brand-building arsenal. It is the Brand Foundation: the formalization of your Brand's essential elements into an unchanging document that serves as the reference point for everything your business ever does.

Yes, ads and marketing communications are an important part of Branding. But nothing is more important than leveraging a Brand Foundation to shape the culture of your organization – to build your Brand from the inside out.

*It's what people think of you™

Brand: It ain't the logo*

*It's what people think of you™

[6] Build a Foundation

To keep your Brand focused, effective and safe from the constant threat of change, it must be formalized and carved in stone.

"Lock your brand in a glass box. Everyone can see it, but only the CEO gets the key."

MacLaren McCann

To help justify their constant tinkering with the Brand, old friends and new friends like to tell themselves that the Brand wasn't carefully thought out in the first place – that the Brand doesn't represent any sort of master plan. So it's no harm done to change it.

Wrong.

The Brand's elements may not have been written down by the founder of the business, or even clearly articulated by her to stakeholders, but I can guarantee you that they were absolutely the product of her original plan.

Unfortunately, when an entrepreneur starts an organization, she doesn't always take time, amid the chaos of getting things up and running, to write down the elements that comprise her Brand. And when the Brand's elements aren't written down from Day 1 – posted for all to see and religiously refer to – the Brand inevitably starts to drift.

It's an especially big problem when the organization grows rapidly and the founder's attention is drawn away from the guiding principles that made her successful in the first place. And it's a huge issue when she is no longer with the organization at all.

A written and unchangeable Brand Foundation communicates clearly to all stakeholders – potential and actual employees, customers, investors, strategic partners, acquisition targets and suitors, the media, everyone – what the Brand stands for. It articulates the Brand's essential components, acts as a single, constant point of reference and drives consistency on everything from employee recruitment to the wording on your website to the color of the paint on your walls.

The Elements of the Brand Foundation Are:

Core Purpose – *Why we exist.*

Vision – *Where we are going, and how we'll know we're there.*

Mission – *What we do every day to get there.*

Values – *What we believe in; our principles.*

Position – *How we make a difference.*

Positioning Statement – *How we say our difference.*

Character – *How we act; our voice.*

Hold it Just One Second

I know what you're thinking: "Wait a minute. Did I see the word "mission" in that Foundation thing?"

Perhaps you are skeptical of mission statements. I am too, when they are guilty of trying to accomplish too much; that makes them too hard for employees to "live." The Brand Foundation, on the other hand, consists of a mission and six other elements. First, because people find it easier to remember seven concise pieces of information than one painfully long sentence. And second, because much of the content found in traditional mission statements doesn't describe the mission at all. In fact this content is actually the vision, position, values and so on.

A written and unchangeable Brand Foundation articulates the Brand's essential components, acts as a single point of reference and drives consistency.

Build the Brand Team

Along with the need to be memorable and precise, another requirement for successful Foundation-building is the involvement of management and staff. Without a significant level of input from a range of employees, getting their buy-in will be difficult or impossible. As noted below, for certain foundational elements it is best to involve employees of all functions and tenures.

Organize these people into a Brand team. It will give them a sense of ownership in the process and its outcome: they'll be much more likely to live the Foundation day in and day out, keeping your Brand consistently lodged in their own minds and those of other stakeholders.

The process used to build the Foundation is not equally democratic for all elements. Some are the sole domain of the CEO. The CEO is in many cases the founder of the organization – and thus is the only person who can say with absolute authority why the organization exists (core purpose) and where it is going (vision). These items aren't something to be decided by committee. They're gut issues for the person leading the enterprise. Even if the CEO is not the owner, he is still the only person in the business with the required 50,000-foot perspective to ultimately articulate its raison d'etre.

The Glass Box

As we saw in the Staples example of Chapter 2, the highest potential of the Brand is to be the operating principle for your entire business. The Brand Foundation can thus be thought of as a locked glass box that protects that operating principle. Everyone can see it, but they can't change it. To keep it ruthlessly consistent, only the CEO gets the key.

The Foundation ensures that internal decision-making will be less affected by outside influences – and for that matter, the personal preferences or agendas of any individual or group. The Foundation gives internal stakeholders the ability to clearly explain to external stakeholders (like the ad agencies and creative people who are so hot to change your Brand) that anything not fitting the Brand Foundation simply won't be done.

The Surrogate Entrepreneur

Entrepreneurs tend to have an instinctive flair for Branding, whether they see their naturally intense focus as Brand-like thinking or not. But ironically, while the Brand Foundation pays tribute to and formalizes the entrepreneur's innate Branding skill, it is the entrepreneur who most needs to get the Foundation down on paper. This is because entrepreneurs are notoriously bad at "scaling": that is, making the jump from being merely successful to truly great in terms of revenue and profitability.

As a business grows, its needs continually change and running it becomes more and more complex. The entrepreneur's attention is dragged away from fanatical adherence to the foundational Brand elements that made her venture an early success.

As the entrepreneur becomes increasingly distracted, the written Brand Foundation performs an invaluable surrogate function. The entrepreneur used to be the main source of Brand discipline. Now the Foundation is the main source. And in cases where the entrepreneur's end game is to sell her company and move on, a consistently communicated, clearly understood Foundation is vitally important to increasing the Brand equity, market value and hence the saleability of the company. The flip side of this coin is that to the ultimate purchaser, a strong Brand Foundation gives the new acquisition a greater chance of success.

And now, explanations and examples of the Brand Foundation elements.

Core Purpose – *Why we exist.*

Every successful organization was started to address a need that the founding entrepreneur had identified in the market and was passionate to fulfill. The core purpose is intended to communicate the organization's reason for being, so that those who identify with it can find greater meaning in their working life. Unlike goals or strategies, the core purpose endures as a perpetual source of guidance.

No founder or CEO runs an organization that exists solely to make lots of money. Even for the richest of the rich, it's always about something greater than that. In *Built to Last,* Jim Collins refers to a BHAG (pronounced BEE-hag), or Big Hairy Audacious Goal. That's what the core purpose is all about. Think Big. Think Hairy. Think Audacious.

People are least happy during their commute to and from work – and while at work.

Having a BHAG is more important than ever, because North Americans are less happy than ever. Happiness has been in steady decline since it peaked in the 1970s, and according to a study conducted by the London School of Economics, only 32% of North Americans are content. People reported being least happy during their commute to and from work and while at work – which means they're unhappy for at least half of their waking lives.

Happiness doesn't depend on acquiring more stuff anymore. Especially for younger members of the workforce, receiving a paycheck just isn't enough to guarantee a great life. The new generation is in pursuit of meaning, and at the heart of a meaningful life is meaningful work. Be prepared to explain how your organization fits this bill.

Finding "the Why"

Why do I come to work every day? And why should anyone join me? These are the crucial questions that leaders must ask themselves. Every organiza-

tion knows *what* they do. Most know *how* they do it. But as Simon Sinek said in a very popular TED Talk on leadership, very few know *why*[3].

With the Baby Boomers starting to retire, the competition for labor is escalating. As a new generation emerges from business schools in pursuit of meaning, it is organizations that know and consistently share the answer to "why" that will have the ability to attract, retain and inspire the best.

IAMGOLD

Organizations like IAMGOLD, a publicly-traded gold mining company with this purpose: *To enrich the lives of all our stakeholders.* While most of us do not associate mining companies with such a lofty core purpose, these folks truly mean ALL stakeholders – not just shareholders.

Here's how most gold mining companies work. They dig up enormous amounts of earth into a giant pile. Then they pour cyanide over the giant pile, and the gold filters out at the bottom. Fifteen years later, the mine is empty and the company is gone. And the people who've lived for genera-tions in the local villages – often in developing countries – are stuck with no jobs, no future, and an environmental atrocity.

Here's how IAMGOLD works. They help the locals build industries that will sustain their standard of living when the gold mine eventually closes and IAMGOLD leaves town. They just think it's the right thing to do. So from the beginning of their engagement with the local community, IAMGOLD determines which industries – anything from lumber to ecotourism – will sustain the locals' standard of living post-mine.

Then IAMGOLD ensures the local children get the appropriate training for running the community's future industry, even shipping them off to British schools.

The leaders of this Brand are passionate about having a long-term, abun-dantly positive effect on the communities in which they mine. And young people get it. Very few universities are teaching mining engineering these days, so mining companies are really battling for the best people. The IAMGOLD core purpose not only helps local communities, it attracts top-notch people to a company that cares.

For its commitment, IAMGOLD has received awards from industry bodies and the national media as one of the most responsible corporations in Canada.

Better Lives

Mary Kay is the cosmetics Brand famous for the pink Cadillacs driven by the top performers among its highly-empowered female sales force of more than two million. From the Mary Kay perspective, makeup is about a lot more than eye shadow and lipstick. The company's core purpose can be de-  scribed as *To build confidence in the women who wear Mary Kay products and the women who sell them.* As founder Mary Kay Ash puts it, "I feel like I'm doing something far more important than just selling cosmetics, I think we're building lives." In further support of its audacious goals, Mary Kay runs a charitable foundation to fight cancer and violence against women.

For most people, the Walmart Brand is about the lowest prices, period. But Walmart's 2011 change of positioning statement, to *Save Money. Live Better.*, is a more accurate, long overdue expression of their core purpose. Way back when, Sam Walton put that purpose like this: "If we work together, we'll lower the cost of living for everyone...we'll give the world an opportunity to see what it's like to save and have a better life."

A "Why" Found

I am proud yet humbled by how the core purpose of Instinct, a boutique firm, has drawn the best and brightest to us. Again that core purpose is:

To advance the sustainability of North American organizations, reinforcing our free enterprise system and ensuring our continued prosperity as a society.

Scott Chapman is our Chief Brand Officer. After reading the first edition of this book, he left a promising career at PepsiCo, where he was managing the marketing strategy for over 15 different beverage Brands, to work here.

And take a pay cut.

He felt a deep and genuine connection to Instinct's core purpose. He says he knows why he and the rest of the Instinct team comes to work every day and understands the real difference we can and do make for the leaders and organizations we work with.

So it looks like our "why" resonates. Does yours?

Vision – *Where we are going, and how we'll know we're there.*

It is the job of the CEO to set an ambitious but achievable goal – one that gives the entire organization a clear and encouraging destination to strive toward.

The vision acts in support of the core purpose and resides in between strategic thinking and the CEO's gut. Like the core purpose, the vision is highly personal. As the leader of the business, the CEO is deeply committed to the vision as the path to organizational success.

Look Up. Way Up.

> I believe that this nation should commit itself to achieving the goal, before this decade is out, of landing a man on the Moon and returning him safely to Earth.

These words, spoken by President John F. Kennedy on May 25th, 1961, are

perhaps the Western world's best-known example of a vision statement. In a single sentence of sparkling clarity, JFK set out the success parameters for an enormously complex project that would consume billions of dollars and the dedicated work of many thousands of Americans. His purpose was to unite the country by demonstrating supremacy over the arch-rival Soviet space program.

Kennedy's call contained the three elements essential to any effective vision. First and foremost, as with a core purpose, it was a BHAG. By setting an ambitiously high bar that can just be reached by the most outstretched of hands, BHAGs energize people to perform at their peak but do not discourage them with the impossible.

Second, JFK's vision was a clear statement of *Where we are going* – "landing a man on the Moon and returning him safely to Earth." While it may seem obvious that visions are about future goals, the "visions" in place at many organizations are actually missions – what we do to *eventually* achieve a vision.

The third essential element of a vision is *How we'll know we're there*. It's vital that stakeholders are able to agree on whether their vision has been reached – so they can unanimously continue to pursue it, or define a new one. JFK had the nerve to set the purely objective standard of (not very much) time – "before this decade is out" – as America's yardstick.

In the 1960s, JFK united a nation – from the top NASA scientist to the average man in the street – behind his audacious vision. The North American leaders of today must aim high if they hope to unify the Brand experience from the executive suite to the shop floor. Take it from a man whose dreams still inspire: ask for the Moon, and you just might get it.

Vision 2020

"By 2020, nobody shall be seriously injured or killed in a new Volvo." For a car company, this remark-ably bold vision, which Volvo calls "Vision 2020," might be every bit as ambitious as JFK's. The plan to achieve it includes integrating preventative and protective safety systems into the car, and developing a better understanding of drivers – because driver behavior is a contributing factor in over 90 percent of all accidents.

"By 2020, nobody shall be seriously injured or killed in a new Volvo."

But don't think you have to be saving lives or literally shooting for the Moon to be aiming high. Reed Hastings, Founder and CEO of Netflix, has said that the vision of his company is to create *The best movie experience. Period.* For Frogbox, which provides moving boxes that are reusable green plastic instead of cardboard, it is *To be the generic term for reusable moving boxes in North America.* The vision for York Central Hospital, a former client, is *To be the finest community hospital in Canada.*

The example of York Central Hospital gives us an opportunity to note that we can't always get the patient to accept treatment. I'm referring to the fact that we pushed hard to convince this client to make their vision time-bound

*It's what people think of you™

– to state with JFK's boldness when they'd know they'd achieved it. But like many clients, they felt they'd be painting themselves into a corner.

Yet that is precisely the point. The idea is to put time pressure on yourself to achieve your vision, not to leave it completely open-ended. A rare few Brands actually define a date by which they will realize their vision. But you don't have to be that specific. A common approach is to say that the recognition of others will define when your vision has been reached. So York Central Hospital's vision could have read *To be recognized by our peers as the finest community hospital in Canada*. The architectural firm Quadrangle, who've designed BMW dealerships among other stunning structures, are another Instinct client. They put a metric on achievement of their vision with the words "of choice" in: *To be the design firm of choice for creating places that inspire.*

As these potent statements suggest, a vision has the most power when it is simply-worded and short – qualities even more important for the mission.

Mission – *What we do every day to get there.*

The mission encompasses the key components of ongoing day-to-day activities that will drive the team toward achieving the vision.

Setting the core purpose and vision is the domain of the CEO. But developing the next element of the Brand Foundation – the mission – is a group activity because it's not by definition a unique motivation that exists only in the CEO's mind. Building the mission should be viewed as a consensus-building opportunity that relies on managers and staff for input on how to run the business every day. Mission development is also an opportunity to secure team alignment with the entire Brand Foundation.

Keep it Simple

Shoe juggernaut Zappos is a Brand with billions in sales and is ranked by *Fortune* magazine as one of America's best companies to work for. Their very concise mission? *To provide the best customer service possible.*

Every Brand mission should strive for such simplicity and power. So simple that employees of every level can read it and quickly know what to focus on every day in their jobs. When developing your mission, make sure you can answer "yes" to this question: if a new employee came into work and discovered everyone was gone for the day, could he simply read the mission and figure out something on-Brand to do?

He could at AtlasCare, a home services company with a more than 80-year history of exceptional customer service. Their mission gives this simple reminder to each and every employee: *We work hard at earning our customers' trust so they proactively refer us.*

Culture = Brand

For Zappos employees to deliver on something so bold, they must be given more than raw tools like free shipping and a one-year return policy – however impressive those tools may be for a shoe company. They must be set up for success with an immersive employment culture ("culture," as you may recall, being the only synonym for "Brand"). As Founder and CEO Tony Hsieh puts it, "If we get the culture right, then everything else, including the customer service, will fall into place."

"If we get the culture right, then everything else will fall into place."

Values – *What we believe in; our principles.*

Values are the non-negotiable, fundamental beliefs you share, which guide you in how you do business and conduct yourselves with all people.

Tony knows that developing and living a strong set of values is essential to getting the culture right. Values are a (usually short) collection of words that capture the Brand's principles. Whereas the core purpose and vision are creations of the CEO's mind, values can be previously held by employees.

Zappos has a very distinct set of values:

1. Deliver WOW Through Service
2. Embrace and Drive Change
3. Create Fun and A Little Weirdness
4. Be Adventurous, Creative, and Open-Minded
5. Pursue Growth and Learning

*It's what people think of you™

6. Build Open and Honest Relationships With Communication
7. Build a Positive Team and Family Spirit
8. Do More With Less
9. Be Passionate and Determined
10. Be Humble

Be Real

Just like all other Foundation elements, the values have to be authentic and practiced faithfully, or your stakeholders will see right through them and dismiss your entire Brand as phony.

If you've ever bought shoes from Zappos, you know their values are the real deal. You definitely know their customer service reps are happy without fail. Less visible may be the Zappos music video, the 430-page culture book and their interview questions – like "How weird are you on a scale from 1-10?" and "What's your theme song?" – that help find the very best Zappos Brand ambassadors.

internal comms ideas

You may have heard this remark-able fact: after completing their training, new employees are offered $2,000 to quit. It's a very gutsy gambit that allows those who remain to make a statement of commitment to their new employer and the values it upholds.

An American Icon

Throughout the life of the organization, the values are ever-present, deeply felt and non-negotiable. They are fundamental to some companies that have lasted a very, very long time. Like Brooks Brothers – the Brand that's dressed generations of families, Hollywood legends, sports greats and military heroes for *almost 200 years*.

As we might expect from an organization vastly more senior than Zappos, their values are more traditional: *Relationships, Innovation, History, Fairness* and *Celebration.*

But Brooks Brothers doesn't exactly creak with age. They continue to bring innovative clothing to market (including the non-iron dress shirt) while honoring their history – demonstrated by acts like supplying

1960s-style clothing to *Mad Men*, a TV program of huge influence in the world of design. Or by having a "Made in America" section of clothing in their stores.

Position – *How we make a difference.*

The position is your unique offering in the marketplace that separates you from competitors. It is a difference that you authentically own.

We've already covered the Brand position – the Foundation element so important it gets a chapter to itself – in Chapter 4. If you like, refer back to it for a refresh, or move onward to the position's outward expression: the positioning statement.

Positioning Statement – *How we say our difference.*

The positioning statement is a creative and more emotional way to communicate the position to stakeholders, and is used next to and in support of the Brand name. A positioning statement is not a "tagline" or "slogan," which by comparison are usually campaign-related, short term and do not embrace the power of the position.

The positioning statement is the unique promise of the Brand, expressed in vocabulary consistent with the character of the Brand (more on character in a moment). Whereas the position is *how we make a difference*, the positioning statement is *how we **say** our difference*. Volvo's position is "safety," and their positioning statement is *For Life*. Subway's position is "healthy," and their positioning statement is *Eat Fresh*.

Not a Tagline

A positioning statement is an articulate expression of the Brand position, not the impermanent, hucksterish slogan implied by the flippant term "tagline." Zipcar's *Wheels when you want them* is a bona fide positioning statement – a dead-on description of a truly awesome business model that gets you a rental car in literal seconds. Gillette's *The Best a Man Can Get* is a classic statement of their legendary commitment to making their own products obsolete in the name of continuous improvement.

Taglines, in contrast, do not reference the Brand's point of difference. They are throwaway messages that hope to convince internal and external stakeholders of something that may not be entirely true. In the United States,

It's what people think of you™

think of *Bank of Opportunity*, the tagline of Bank of America – an institution facing lawsuits for illegal fees, and that the Treasury Department says is America's slowest at responding to mortgage requests. In Canada, think of Bell's *Today just got better.* Ask yourself: when was the last time Bell made your day better?

Taglines do nothing to reinforce the Brand with stakeholders. Worse, they invite mockery because they're just unsupported wishful thinking. Positioning statements, on the other hand, reinforce the essence of the Brand with everyone. Craft yours by working hard to crystallize your unique Brand position, and then, in a few choice words, communicate it to the world.

We don't just pick a positioning statement we "like."

The Positioning Statement Has Jobs to Do

Get the process started by embracing the fact that choosing a positioning statement is, for the most part, not a subjective matter. We don't just pick one we "like." Instead, we must ask if it does a defined list of jobs (jobs very similar to those done by all great names, as discussed in Chapter 15). If not, it gets eliminated from consideration.

A Long-Term Investment

The positioning statement is not something you change on a quarterly basis under investor pressure, for a new ad campaign or because the marketing department is bored. The positioning statement is a long-term strategic investment in your Brand that doesn't get changed unless your Brand position changes. And that, of course, would only be as part of a profound change in the Brand's strategic direction, considered with painstakingly profound care.

Character – *How we act; our voice.*

Your character attributes are an internal guide to how you want to be perceived, so that everything you say and do is carried out consistently by those who represent your Brand.

*It's what people think of you™

Although it is the component most often overlooked when building a Brand Foundation, the character influences everything. The character is the piece that dictates how the firm will consistently communicate. Will it be with humor, seriousness or sophistication? Will it be friendly, authoritative or refined? These are questions for which a range of management and staff are capable of providing insight.

A Brand's character is communicated in personal interactions among internal and external Brand stakeholders. It also takes the form of more tangible Brand communication like product packaging, product design, service delivery, vocabulary and the overall visual identity on pieces like signage, letterhead and marketing collateral.

One of my favorite character examples comes from Veritas Communications, a top public relations firm whose long client list includes Target, Subway, Canada Dry and Motts. These people are seriously energetic. Their vision includes a commitment *To live and die by the strength of our people and our ideas.* Their mission is *To tackle everything like a defining moment.* So maybe it's no surprise that their character is *connected, unconventional, clever, proven, ready,* and my favorite, *caffeinated.* Veritas visually expresses these traits by printing them on Branded coffee mugs and their firetruck-red boardroom walls.

A Diamond in the Rough

By expressing themselves with a character aligned with the other elements of their Brand Foundation, Veritas gets the most bang for their communications buck. Yet there are many organizations that hobble their marketing and advertising efforts by conveying a character that doesn't jive with their overall Brand. Spence Diamonds, a retailer in Canada and the state of Texas, provides an especially jarring example.

In Spence's radio ads, CEO Sean Jones portrays himself as a total buffoon, babbling excitedly and howling strangely. He proudly refers to himself as annoying and even speculates, on his company website, that someone might want to punch him in the nose.

The ads definitely don't suggest the shopping experience you want when buying an incredibly important item you know nothing about.

*It's what people think of you™

So when a friend suggested I "ignore those ads" and check out what he described as a great experience, I was skeptical. And then pleasantly surprised: Spence delivered a remark-able experience by building enormous trust – by smoothly guiding me through the selection process, educating me about cut, clarity, colour and carat, and allowing me to select and inspect my diamond using a binocular microscope. An experience run by jokers, this was not.

Be sure to observe the number one rule of Branding – be consistent – by aligning the character of your communications with the character of the buying experience you provide. Here we have clownish ads that scare away anyone looking for an in-store experience that creates confidence. It's a needless waste of corporate resources that hides their Brand's remark-ability.

Everyone's Job

It's the job of every employee to live the Brand every day, in everything they do. Constant referral to the Foundation ensures this consistency and helps prevent old friends and new friends from wasting your money, time and hard-won Brand equity.

But one individual has more responsibility than the others: the CEO. The more the CEO talks about the Brand Foundation and how it applies to everyone's job, the more effective the organization will be at delivering the Brand day after day.

[7] Be the CBO

Because the Brand lives and dies
with the actions of every employee,
it's got to be owned by the CEO – the
only person with the power to make
delivering it everyone's responsibility.

"In the end, authentic brand management
boils down to understanding that a brand is
a promise that has to be fulfilled everywhere,
at any time. So when something doesn't fit,
you must make sure that it isn't done."

Helmut Panke
Former Chairman
BMW

Because a Brand is what people think of you, it lives and dies with the behavior of every single employee. Every touchpoint matters. And when every touchpoint matters, the Brand is much too big and important to be the responsibility of the marketing department alone. Yet today, in the great majority of North American companies, not-for-profits and government departments, marketing carries the Brand mantle all by itself.

Instead, the Brand must be owned by the top executive, who often has the title of CEO. The CEO is the only person with the power to make the job of delivering the Brand everyone's responsibility. Thus the CEO must be the CBO – the Chief Brand Officer.

CBOs articulate the elements of the Brand Foundation over and over again, to motivate their people to deliver remark-able products, services and experiences. CBOs find the power to continually relate the Foundation to everyone's work in a passionate, convincing and compelling way. So that everyone can see how their work, whether exciting or mundane, contributes to delivering the Brand to stakeholders at every touchpoint.

CBOs find the power to continually relate the Foundation to everyone's work in a passionate, convincing and compelling way.

Repeat After Me:

I spend a lot of time telling CEOs to talk about their Brand Foundation. The most common response I get? "I told everybody in the firm just last summer." Or, "They're going to go crazy if I talk about the Foundation again next month!"

Wrong answers.

John P. Kotter of Harvard Business School has researched why so many change initiatives fail in major corporations[4]. He cites eight errors commonly made by organizational leaders attempting change – and they apply perfectly to Brand initiatives, regardless of organization size.

*It's what people think of you™

Kotter finds that a key characteristic of failed change initiatives is "under-communicating the vision by a factor of 10." His use of "vision" here is analogous to our use of "Brand Foundation."

The executives who are effective at making change, however, "incorporate [messages about the vision] into their hour-by-hour activities":

> In a routine discussion about a business problem, they talk about how the proposed solutions fit (or don't fit) into the bigger picture. In a regular performance appraisal, they talk about how the employee's behavior helps or undermines the vision. In a review of a division's quarterly performance, they talk not only about the numbers but also about how the division's executives are contributing to the transformation. In a routine Q&A with employees at a company facility, they tie their answers back to renewal goals.

Those leaders most successful at making change "use all existing communication channels to broadcast the vision":

> They turn boring and unread company newsletters into lively articles about the vision. They take ritualistic and tedious quarterly management meetings and turn them into exciting discussions of the transformation. They throw out much of the company's generic management education and replace it with courses that focus on business problems and the new vision. The guiding principle is simple: use every possible channel, especially those that are being wasted on non-essential information[5].

So, I want to hear more CEOs say this to me: "I was in a meeting yesterday and reminded everyone about our values, and then asked how everyone is aligning their activities to them." Or: "I just asked our office manager to clean up the reception area closet, because our vision is to be the leading accounting firm, and all the junk piled up in there says bad things about our attention to detail."

Or: "I'm making sure that our new office conveys our Brand Foundation even better than our last digs." I am referring to the CBO leadership of Beverley Hammond, CEO of Veritas Communications: the PR firm with *caffeinated* as a character trait. It was truly wonderful to learn that, when they moved to a new space, they briefed the architect on their Brand Foundation to ensure it was brought to life in the new environment. I can tell you they did an incredibly beautiful job.

People Need a Reminder

When the people in your organization fall short of delivering the Brand, it's not because they're not smart. It's just that in the chaos of the workday, people forget that the handling (or mishandling) of every little detail gets everyone closer to (or farther away from) a common, larger goal. That's why the Brand Foundation must be communicated over and over again in ways that relate to everyone's daily work. Even if you think your staff is motivated only by money, try giving them a relevant, well-articulated Foundation to work with – and you'll see that they actually work for a higher reward.

Just Say No

Helmut Panke, past Chairman of BMW, understands what being a Chief Brand Officer is all about. Helmut understands that ownership of the Brand must emanate from the highest level of the enterprise. That's the only way the Brand can remain true and consistent throughout the organization.

For Panke, CBO-style leadership is insurance in favor of doing the right things and insurance against doing the wrong things. Asked in an interview about his special responsibilities for maintaining and building the Brand, Panke answered that the biggest task was to say "no":

> In the end, authentic brand management boils down to understanding that a brand is a promise that has to be fulfilled everywhere, at any time. So when something doesn't fit, you must make sure that it isn't done.

Asked to recall the last significant time he said "no," he replayed the debate as to whether BMW should be in the minivan market.

> We don't have a van because a van as it is in the market today, does not fulfill any of the BMW brand values. Take any of the BMW brand products, sit in them, touch it, feel it, hear it, feel the feedback from the road. You know exactly this is what a BMW feels like. Someone said a brand is only skin deep. No it's not. It has to be authentic, through everything you do.

CEOs: take your lead from Helmut. Don't leave Brand responsibility with somebody else (e.g. the marketing department), or you'll distance yourself from your proper CBO role. Without your constant sponsorship from the top, none of the other departments will give the Brand the careful attention and support it requires.

Cars that People Love

I've taken my share of shots at Ford, but I tip my hat to Alan Mulally, who's been a terrific CBO in turning them around. America once had a love affair with cars, including Ford models like the Mustang and Thunderbird. Then Ford broke our hearts. Year after year, it was a crushing disappointment to see Ford disrespecting us with bad models. Those who continued to buy them did so out of a twisted sense of national duty.

Enter Mulally. He narrowed down the number of models at Ford, and brought the company back to making cars people – lots of people – actually want. It's almost a shock seeing up-wardly mobile folks buy Ford SUVs – not BMW, Acura, Honda or any number of other happening Brands – for their young families. Which, pre-turnaround, would have been unthinkable. Credit Mr. Mulally for playing Cupid.

Good Things Growing...

One of my most dedicated CBOs is Rob Clark, CEO of PICKSEED. Later on, you'll see that PICKSEED provides the seed for some of the sporting world's most storied grass surfaces. Rob fully embraces his role as CBO, and I love reading the emails in which he relates everything back to the Brand Foundation.

Check out these excerpts from an email in which Rob was reviewing some ad artwork. Keep in mind that one of PICKSEED's values is *Integrity*.

- Three photos are out of focus and the one that isn't, isn't very remark-able
- Replace "Trust" with "Integrity" to tie to Brand Foundation

Even a remark-ability reference! Way to go, Rob.

Branding Can Be This Comfortable

TD Canada Trust is an inspiring tale of CBO leadership, first by Ed Clark and then (fitting for a Canadian bank) Tim Hockey. In the late 90s, Toronto-Dominion Bank found themselves dead last among the "Big Five" Canadian banks. Like the others, they opened late, closed early and were otherwise a pain to deal with.

*It's what people think of you™

Then they realized they needed a culture (i.e. Brand) change. So they bought a smaller bank, Canada Trust, to absorb it and learn from it. Canada Trust was the veritable anti-bank: *they were even open in the morning and at night.*

Fast-forward more than 10 years. TD Canada Trust (TD) has flirted with being the largest Canadian bank by capitalization. It's very much due to the brilliant consistency with which they've delivered on their positioning statement – *Banking can be this comfortable* – in every aspect of the banking experience.

For example, TD continues to shape the terms of competition on operating hours – opening at 8am, closing at 8pm, staying open on Saturdays. RBC tried to take a page from the TD playbook by opening on Saturdays. So now TD is open Saturdays *and* Sundays.

And they've unveiled a new, modernized branch environment called "Bravo," designed to create a welcoming, comfortable place that customers actually enjoy visiting. A place with an open layout, a play area for kids, free coffee, rooms for community use, web kiosks, video-conferencing with banking experts and more. It's the physical embodiment of the Brand position.

But TD's most recognizable emblem of comfort is clearly its cushy green chair, which the company has used with wonderful consistency in its advertising, and with brilliant creativity in a host of other applications. Consider just this one example: TD's sponsorship of a "moderated conversation" between former U.S. Presidents Bill Clinton and George W. Bush. The past Commanders-in-Chief appeared at the Metro Toronto Convention Centre to chat about life after the White House, and to handle with trademark Southern ease some direct challenges of their records from Frank McKenna, former Canadian Ambassador to the United States.

Media coverage of the event was worldwide. And what every account reported was that these two men looked relaxed. At ease. Comfortable.

This was an ingeniously engineered piece of Brand messaging. No need to plaster the TD logo all over the place: instead they simply sat each man in a humongous, comfortable green leather chair.

No, it wasn't the chairs themselves that relaxed these two men – relief from

*It's what people think of you™

the burdens of leading the free world can explain that easily enough – but it's nearly impossible to look agitated while sitting in a chair so deep, you're practically lying down. Branding, indeed, can be this comfortable.

At Instinct, we've never forgotten that the guy at RBC was very unhelpful when we first signed up with them. Since that time, we've been so impressed by TD's Brand consistency that we switched to them. We aren't surprised that our TD guy is a complete contrast to the RBC fellow: we'd heard that TD's hiring managers dig especially hard to see how candidates will exceed customer expectations. Plus, our new guy has a nice trophy in his office with a little green chair on top – a standard symbol of recognition for TD employees who go above and beyond.

Consistency Rolls Downhill

Considered all together, this is the kind of consistency that can only come when the CEO is acting as CBO – as the single person with the 50,000-foot view of the Brand and the authority to ensure everyone lives it every day in every action.

One word of criticism for CBO Tim Hockey: the architects designing your stores have too much power. Believe it or not, there are no green chairs in your retail branches or even in the new Bravo format.

Jobs on the Job

Steve Jobs was the quintessential Chief Brand Officer. His story was also the classic example of how firms lose sight of their original Brand Foundation and can get screwed up by the professional, non-CBO executive who replaces the founder. As you probably know, Jobs co-founded Apple Computer, but was fired in the 1980s by the board and president of his own hiring.

From the beginning, his vision was to create "perfect" machines[6]. Fulfilling this vision meant building hardware, software and everything else in-house. The beautiful aesthetics and superb usability of Apple products are the result. They form the basis of Apple's stature as one of the world's most recognizable Brands – a Brand that is not just appreciated, but actually loved. A Brand that has sold half a billion iPods, iPhones and iPads – and counting.

When Jobs made his triumphant return to the top job in 1997, Apple stock was trading in the three dollar range. Five days before Jobs' death in 2011, it was trading at $381.45, an increase of more than 10,000%. Words truly cannot do justice to CBO leadership that strong.

A Brand Adrift

Although Apple was having financial problems before Jobs left, the Brand really went off the rails in his absence. The replacement CEOs went off-vision and drove the company almost to bankruptcy.

The third of these replacements, Gil Amelio, described an undisciplined corporate culture and fragmentation – a running off in all directions – still in place from the years of replacement CEO #1. Amelio's reference to corporate culture really catches my attention, because of course the only synonym for "Brand" is "culture." So what Amelio was really saying, perhaps without realizing it, was that the Apple Brand was adrift – that it didn't have a CBO to keep it moored.

From the beginning, his vision was to create "perfect" machines.

Andy Hertzfeld was a member of the original development team behind Apple's Macintosh computer. Commenting in 1996, before Jobs' return, he absolutely saw things from the CBO perspective:

> Apple never recovered from losing Steve; Steve was the heart and soul and driving force; it would be quite a different place today; they lost their soul[7].

Returned to the CEO's chair as Amelio's replacement, Jobs quickly yanked Apple back to its "perfect" vision and gave the Brand its first big hit in years – the stunning iMac series of personal computers. He also killed a licensing agreement, the first ever signed by Apple, that would have allowed hardware manufacturers to produce the Apple operating system. Jobs feared that "Mac knockoffs" would weaken the Apple Brand.

In other words, that they'd block achievement of the vision.

*It's what people think of you™

Jay Forbes

One of the best CBOs I've worked with is Jay Forbes, when he was president and CEO of Aliant, a provider of phone, mobile, digital TV and Internet services in Atlantic Canada. Aliant had just completed an $11 billion merger with BCE, doubling the size of the company overnight.

Aliant's vision under Jay was to be the company with the closest connection to the hearts and minds of Atlantic Canadians. Jay had a constant and total focus on conceptualizing all company activities as being about the vision and other elements of Aliant's Brand Foundation. At each and every talk he gave to his people, he related the subject matter back to it – sometimes asking the question of his audience explicitly: how does this relate to our vision? Our mission? Our position? And so on.

At 6am every Monday, Jay would send his staff their first email of the week. In it, he would report his personal schedule for every day in the week ahead, and how his planned activities related to achieving the company vision. On Monday he might be meeting with government regulators to help change policy for their product, hosting customers at a noon lunch and handing out awards to the local Brownie troop that evening. Then he'd tell a story from the week before, about a staff member who had done something special.

He'd give the same preview for every day that week. Why? To explain how these activities were helping everyone achieve the shared vision. In doing so, Jay was demonstrating the most critical aspects of Brand Foundation management: Have a Brand Foundation, talk about it, and then keep talking about it.

Brand: It ain't the logo*

*It's what people think of you™

[8] Marketers: Surrender Your Brand

If the marketing department truly wants the organization to live and breathe the Brand, they've got to give it up – to the CBO.

"Everything we touch, we shift.
And everything we shift, we make better."

Nissan

Imagine that due to a recession, cost cuts are required at Volvo. There's no way around it: some feature has to be chopped from next year's models. The guys in the accounting department are trying to figure out what. Hey – maybe it should be a side airbag!

If Volvo's CEO is an effective CBO, it's a no-brainer for accounting: they would rather remove their right arms than an airbag, because it's been drilled into their heads that all things safety, including airbags, are absolutely crucial to Volvo's position. Scary as it sounds, with a weak or non-existent CBO in charge, the accounting boys won't draw a very strong connection between protecting the Brand and what they do on a daily basis. The Brand? Doesn't the marketing department usually handle that? And the side airbag is one step closer to the trash can.

Does this sound unlikely to you? That someone in the Volvo organization could be so dim as to threaten the Brand's precious safety position?

The Brand? Doesn't the marketing department usually handle that?

An Accident

Consider this. Years back, a friend's wife was in a harrowing traffic accident. She was on the highway and rolled the family van – with their new baby in the back seat. Mom and child were properly strapped in, thank goodness, and other than a few bruises and the emotional shakeup associated with this kind of event, they were OK. But the deeply unnerving experience was sudden and profound inspiration to go out and buy a Volvo.

The model purchased by my friend and his wife had a few mechanical issues. Nevertheless, the dealership service was attentive and concerned. So concerned, in fact, that they tried to atone with a very expensive gift – a large mechanical corkscrew. I must point out that the Volvo-Branded box in which it came said "Don't drink and drive" – but did I mention it was a corkscrew?

We all have a sense of the horrible toll that impaired driving inflicts on our society. Mothers Against Drunk Driving (MADD) tells us that almost 19,000 North Americans (yes, that is nineteen thousand) are killed each year in alcohol-related car accidents. So why would a company that has devoted more than 80 years to driving safety, that has been responsible for virtually every safety feature innovation on every automobile today, even come close to associating its name with booze?

The corkscrew incident is a sobering reminder that even the most consistent Brands can wobble. To keep this truism top of mind, the Volvo corkscrew is prominently displayed in the Brand "museum" we maintain at Instinct.

If Volvo hopes to avoid more corkscrew incidents, Volvo's CEO had better convince his dealerships that, contrary to popular opinion, the Brand is not the job of the marketing department alone. It is the responsibility of everyone in the organization. And only the constantly engaged CBO can make it so.

Marketers: Surrender Your Brand

"I'm here to take away your responsibility for the Brand."

If they inquire about my presence at an industry event, that's what I say to marketing managers, the people that bear almost exclusive responsibility for Brand management at the great majority of organizations.

I wait for their heads to snap back.

I go on to explain that a Brand is not the logo. It's not the website. And it's sure not the advertising they're blowing all their money on. I tell them – and you may be surprised to hear this – that a Brand is what people think of you.

Every time your Brand comes in contact with your employees, customers and all the other stakeholders out there, they judge you. This means that all the hard work and all the money that marketers spend on advertising and promotion is pointless if the entire organization isn't out there every day doing what these communications say it will.

The marketing managers I talk to often feel ineffective and frustrated, because without the permission of the CEO, trying to get everyone in their organization to fulfill the Brand promise is next to impossible. They can walk down to the loading dock to chat with the transport manager about painting the trucks in Brand colors – because the trucks are a fantastically effective way of getting the Brand message out there – but the transport guy will protest that he'll have to wash the trucks and paint them when it's time to sell them. He doesn't "get it" because the CEO hasn't explained to him how important his job is in the context of the Brand.

Beyond Paid Bragging

When I talk about CBO leadership, the marketers quickly see the positive implications: "You mean you're going to get me permission from my CEO to permeate Brand thinking into every nook and cranny of this organization? You mean I can be more than just the logo cop?" But many marketers don't want to hear about it. They're happy making advertising – so what if what their ads promise doesn't get delivered at the front end?

Shift. Sort Of.

Consider Nissan. I think the kaizen-like premise of their "Shift" campaign is brilliant: "Everything we touch, we shift. And everything we shift, we make better." Set against this, I was intrigued that Nissan Finance didn't ask a friend to renew her Altima lease until four weeks before it expired. Naturally she'd already made other plans with a competitor – Mazda.

Only the CEO has the weight to drive on-Brand behavior throughout your organization.

Yet she'd very recently taken her Altima in for service at the dealership. Why didn't the service guys – who knew darn well that the lease was expiring – walk her into the showroom and get her talking to a salesperson? "Everything we shift, we make better," right?

Not entirely. "Shift" was no doubt created by the smart folks at Nissan marketing, but the campaign hasn't been effectively communicated to employees beyond their four walls. I had one of my Brand Coaches phone some Nissan people to see if they understood what "Shift" meant – if they were able to articulate the Brand promise and, more importantly, deliver it.

They weren't. The receptionist at a local dealership answered that "Shift" meant, "Shifting gears – I believe it's just like standard and automatic gears." A salesman at the same location advised, "We're not running that ad anymore. But 'Shift' means getting into gear with Avenue Nissan." A phone call to the

*It's what people think of you™

"Customer Satisfaction" line posted on the Nissan website was another wrong number. Literally: "To be honest sir, I'd be guessing to answer that for you. This is Nissan Finance. Nissan Inc. can answer that for you." And to cap it all off: "Yes, I know the wrong number is on our website – I wish they'd correct it: I get five of these calls every day."

Nissan has great products. And great ideas. The crucial missing piece is CBO-inspired leadership.

To all the marketing managers out there: this is the kind of stuff that makes you insane. You just don't have the leverage to drive on-Brand behavior throughout your organization. Only the CEO has the weight to do that. Convince him or her to accept the responsibility for doing so. Because you'll only get the help you need when your CEO becomes a full-fledged CBO.

That's when your job will get truly exciting. Instead of butting heads on the loading dock, just imagine transport – or finance, or purchasing – coming to you and asking, "How can we help live the Brand?"

Brand: It ain't the logo*

*It's what people think of you™

[9] Listen to Your Stakeholders

Ask your stakeholders what they think of you. It takes humility, but it's the most cost-effective and underrated way to take your business to the next level.

"The larger the organization, the more executives tend to insulate themselves from customers."

Ian Wiley
Fast Company

Tom LaSorda, past CEO of Chrysler, got quite a surprise from one of his neighbors. They were chatting over the fence one day when this fellow said to him, "You guys have no clue what your cars are like. You only drive brand new cars!" The neighbor was right on the money. Sure enough, the top people at Chrysler were frequently trading in their cars for fresh new models.

So what did Tom do – force a smile and ignore his pesky neighbor? No. He ordered his senior team to get cars just coming off three-year leases, so they could find out exactly what their customers were experiencing after the post-purchase honeymoon. It's a great credit to Mr. LaSorda that he had the humility to listen to a customer – one of the easiest, cheapest and definitely most cost-effective things you can do to better your Brand. Yet it's one of the most underused.

 Very few organizations look at the little things that could cement the loyalty of an existing customer and turn him into a Brand evangelist. They're locked in a continual search for the next big thing to attract new customers. But we all know that getting new customers is – what, seven times? 10 times? – more expensive than keeping the ones you already have.

I'm not talking about doing massive, complex, time-consuming and expensive research programs. On the contrary. I'm saying there's tremendous value to be had in simply speaking with and listening to your customers on a regular basis.

The BlackBerry "Prayer"

My favorite monthly read is *Fast Company* magazine. They once ran a wonderful article about how a young expert on Brand experience took the crusty bankers at Credit Suisse through an investigative process to see the bank from the customer's perspective[8].

The lad didn't do it with million-dollar market research, but with simple observation and actually talking to customers. As he opened his presentation, 200 of the senior bankers were fiddling with their BlackBerrys – bent over in the "BlackBerry prayer," as they say. These execs didn't seem the least bit interested...until our hero announced he was going to call the Credit Suisse customer service line LIVE from the podium. The fear on the bankers' faces was unmistakable: they didn't have a clue what the experience was going to be like.

*It's what people think of you™

Our Brand experience expert later began an immersion program in which he took Credit Suisse executives to three branches: the first simply to observe customers in action, the second to perform a typical customer task (currency exchange), and the third branch to ask customers questions and use the website to check out current mortgage rates.

The executives realized that in some cases, they were making it hard for customers to do business with them. On the basis of the immersion program, they quickly undertook a number of initiatives in a bid to improve customer service. Two of the three branches visited were being redesigned, and programs to reduce wait times were implemented.

Where's My Bank Again?

I once did something similar with the senior brass of BMO's online brokerage service, InvestorLine. It was, and remains, a top-ranked service. Their CEO at the time, Tom Flanagan, was a true CBO. I asked him and a group of the bank's executives to meet me at a BMO bank branch I had picked, mere blocks from BMO's head office.

Two of the executives sent me emails telling me no such branch existed. Ultimately I persuaded them to meet me at the coordinates and see for themselves.

InvestorLine had been trying to get branch managers to refer qualified retail banking clients to their service. I'd convinced Tom to abstain from an outside advertising campaign because our research indicated that the largest cohort of new customers was coming from within the BMO organization: they were retail banking customers adopting InvestorLine's services. So the branch managers had been given posters, displays and brochures to help them make referrals to InvestorLine. Unfortunately, the branch managers had been less than cooperative: as the branch visit clearly demonstrated, the InvestorLine promotional materials had been less than prominently displayed and were too hard to find.

Of course, none of these executives had ever gone into a branch to look for their own Brand collateral. They had simply developed the stuff in the vacuum of their corporate offices and didn't understand the environment the materials had to live and work in. How did they expect to effectively coach the branch managers if they hadn't been into a branch to see for themselves what was going on?

*It's what people think of you™

Kyu and QUEUE

Kyu Lee is a man who knows exactly what's going on with his Brand. He is CEO of QUEUE, an IT services and support company. Kyu calls himself CBO and keeps himself and everyone else focused on the Brand position: *Extraordinary service experiences.* Experiences like the flawless switching out of the 2,000 personal computers of a leading consulting firm in a single weekend. And photographing each desk beforehand so that all was left exactly as it was found. All by technicians that wear suits and ties instead of jeans. Says Kyu:

> We need to stay remark-able. We use a (short, two-minute) survey with our clients, and ask them to give examples of remark-able experiences they've received. The results come directly to me, and the clients love it. One small change we've made among many is sending cookie baskets to clients at key touchpoints, as recognition and thanks. It is right on Brand for us.

Listening to your stakeholders is that simple.

Oxford

Oxford Properties, at the time North America's largest manager of prime retail and office real estate, contacted me amidst a wave of acquisitions in their industry. Oxford found its offering commoditized – different in no meaningful way from its competition – but then-CEO Jon Love wanted to capitalize on the acquisition rush and be purchased next. Unable to afford "granite and steel" changes that might raise the value of its 120 office towers, Oxford's skeptical management team decided to give Brand Coaching a chance.

Because of high tenant turnover, Oxford was spending $25 million annually in real estate fees. In addition were the opportunity costs of units sitting empty between customers, and repairs prior to putting new tenants in place. By talking to Oxford tenants, we discovered that the source of the high turnover was a landlord-tenant relationship so distant, so adversarial, that most tenants didn't even know who to call when they had a problem with the air conditioning, a burnt-out light bulb, whatever. It became clear that if Oxford could do a better job of building relationships with its customers, they might manage to keep them and substantially increase the company's value.

Funny Business

When it comes to the matter of customer relationship management, commercial real estate is a funny business. Other industries are falling over themselves to form relationships with their customers. But landlords, who actually live with their customers, use a lawyer and a baseball bat to negotiate lease agreements for five, 10, 15 years and do everything they can NOT to build a positive relationship.

Oxford became very much an exception. To meet their goal of redefining the way tenants think of their "landlord," Oxford adopted the positioning statement *Building Relationships* as part of transforming the stale landlord-tenant vocabulary. In the process, they became the first commercial real estate firm in North America to refer to their tenants as – wait for it – "customers."

Oxford also stopped hiring anyone that had ever worked in real estate. New employees were hired on the basis of their talent for customer care. This fresh wave of workers came from backgrounds in nursing, customer service and from big farm families.

Then we launched 310-maxx, a call center and website built into "maxx" – an animated custodian character who represented superb service delivery in all Oxford buildings. The launch campaign involved Internet portals, in-building events and even live mascots.

Only three months after introduction of 310-maxx, over 89% of building occupants knew how to contact their property manager (up from 0.5%!). The volume of incoming phone calls surpassed 1,000 a day. Even tenants in buildings not managed by Oxford were calling 310-maxx asking for the service.

Based on an invigorated Brand that listened to its customers and took action, Oxford sold its business, 11 months after introduction of 310-maxx, for $150 million above net asset value.

Focus Groups?

When we interviewed Oxford's customers, we did not do focus groups. I don't believe in focus groups. I don't think they work. I think they're way overrated and create misinformation. Groups are always hijacked by the most verbose person in attendance, who is very often the least insightful. You end up with one idiot's opinion. And on another level, these mass events are a nightmare to orchestrate – trying to get everyone you want in the same spot at the same time.

I don't believe in focus groups. I don't think they work.

ThinkAudit™

Instinct's approach is to conduct one-on-one conversations with a variety of stakeholders – what we call a ThinkAudit™. We interviewed Oxford customers using this method. A Brand is what people think of you, so exactly what do people think of you? That's the fundamental question of the ThinkAudit. The answers are powerful. The learning is used – together with a clear picture of what you want people to think – to build the client's Brand Foundation.

The ThinkAudit is a simple but highly effective qualitative research technique that draws its strength from the diversity of stakeholders engaged in a brief but candid dialogue about the Brand. On the subject of candor, it's essential that an objective third party conduct the ThinkAudit. Almost always, stakeholders want to help. But equally, they are rarely candid with the Brand owners themselves. Customers, for example, will almost inevitably have at least some issues with your organization and are actually grateful – sometimes downright relieved – for an opportunity to speak anonymously about it.

The ThinkAudit has elements in common with 360° feedback, the method by which employees and managers in a business unit rate each other's performance. But as you'll see, the ThinkAudit yields much richer, more actionable data.

360° Feedback is More Like 120° Feedback

One-on-one interviews are scheduled between Brand Coaches and stake-holders drawn from three categories – employees, customers and strategic partners. Within each of these categories are people with different perspectives based on their role and relationship with the Brand and length of tenure – new, mid-term, long-term and departed. The ThinkAudit thereby creates what we call a holographic image of stakeholder opinion (a holograph being a three-dimensional image projected in empty space by a series of lasers situated at different angles around it). Compared to the ThinkAudit, 360° feedback is more like 120° feedback – because of its reliance on opinions from just one stakeholder group: employees.

A Brand is what people think of you. So, exactly what do people think of you?

Intersection Points

Interviews are crafted to be no more than 14 minutes in length, in order to elicit unadulterated opinions and respect respondents' time. They are conducted in person or over the phone and follow a simple discussion guide. The Brand Coaches are looking for the common thoughts about the Brand – the powerful intersection points of all inputs coming from all interviewees.

We want to know, for example, if they can describe how our client is unique in one word, whether they would recommend this Brand as a place to work and whether they're an organization they'd do business with or invest in.

The responses to these and other lines of inquiry are compiled and analyzed for commonalities. A clear understanding of what people think of the Brand, today, takes shape. Opportunities and barriers to forward progress are identified. Conclusions are drawn and recommendations are made in a presentation to the client's senior team for building the Brand going forward, starting with a Brand Foundation.

The ThinkAudit gives you clarity on what your Brand really is, and how to make it what you want it to be.

*It's what people think of you™

And there's a bonus: the very act of asking your stakeholders for their opinions gives them a very positive impression of your Brand. Clearly you care what they think. That's especially helpful if you haven't been on the best terms lately. All you have to do is make sure to act on any shortcomings they voice.

It's also a reality that sometimes insights from the ThinkAudit can profoundly change top leadership's view of the organization's direction, who should be in what roles, and even who should be with the organization, period. At one investment firm we worked with, the CEO left the day-to-day to become Chairman. At another, the president left completely.

It's an Experience, Not a Motor

Honda's outboard motor division was another ThinkAudit client. Honda being an engineering company, their communications people thought of their motors in almost strictly technical terms. Brand collateral was heavy on charts and diagrams of fuel injectors and hi-rise camshafts. But the customer portion of the ThinkAudit revealed the need for something quite different.

Owners of Honda outboards didn't want to know it was a machine at all. These guys worked hard for 50 weeks a year so they could spend one or two glorious weeks fishing. Machines have a funny way of breaking down – and these fellows didn't want even the mere thought of a mechanical problem to ruin their joyous anticipation.

So we threw out the diagrams and did a series of beautifully-shot ads that fully embraced customer emotions. With images and prose of a guy heading down to the lake with his fishing rod in hand at 6am…the pristine wilderness and the mirror-smooth water…the sound of the tackle box on the dock… the silence undisturbed by the quietest outboard on the planet.

Madonna…

In their attempts to understand how someone with an average voice and dance moves could remain a global pop icon for the better part of 30 years, pundits are fond of saying that Madonna has continually "reinvented" herself. I see it more as a Brand evolution, however. Madonna has in fact avoided revolution: her music has changed over the years, but the key Brand elements – sex and controversy – have always been present.

*It's what people think of you™

We can still make out the ebbs and flows of her career, though. Every several years, Madonna breaks through with a new hairstyle, provocative outfit, clothing line, book, movie, CD or controversial public statement. It always follows the kind of down period encountered by every Brand. And with her resurfacing comes a renewed wave of popularity and revenue.

...and Her Curve

Bruce Mau, author of *Massive Change*, describes this phenomenon as a success trajectory that is common to all industries and businesses. He calls it the "Madonna Curve." The key for Brands is to realize when the downward portion of the Curve is underway, make the right adjustments, and redouble efforts to move the Brand onward and upward.

We apply a similar type of thinking at Instinct. Over time, business environments change. As a result, the way that stakeholders think of even the best-managed Brand will change as well. I've found that after about three years, stakeholder perceptions can become diffused and your Brand's growth may plateau.

It could be that you've entered a new market or that your competitive landscape has changed. Or maybe you've been involved in a merger or acquisition, been challenged with attracting and retaining top talent, or been delivering inconsistent stakeholder experiences.

Whatever the reason for the change in your environment, this is the time to do a ThinkAudit and then revitalize your Brand. To make an evolutionary (not revolutionary) course correction and a fresh twist – one that will drive the Brand in a renewed upward trajectory through its next phase of growth.

Get Out There

I once worked with a group of corporate jewellery stores, whose biggest fear was the threat posed by independent owner/operators. Every December, while the independents were helping out in their stores, working the cash register and getting to know their customers during the busiest season of the year, the corporate boys were locked up at head office worrying about Easter, still three months down the road.

Instead of worrying about the future, get out there and listen now. No matter what your stakeholders say, you'll find comfort in knowledge – honest.

Brand: It ain't the logo*

*It's what people think of you™

[10] Evolution, Not Revolution

The only thing tougher than establishing your stakeholders' thoughts is changing them. But when change is absolutely unavoidable, please: don't do anything rash.

"We have a lot of people revolutionizing the world because they've never had to present a working model."

Charles F. Kettering

A Brand is what people think of you. And with the multitude of messages hitting your target market, the only thing tougher than establishing your target's thoughts is changing them.

But sometimes change is absolutely unavoidable. When it is, make like Madonna and let *evolution, not revolution* be your mantra.

Fairmont Hotels & Resorts

When Canadian Pacific Hotels & Resorts bought Fairmont Hotels in 1999, they picked up some of the most legendary hotel properties in the world – including the Fairmont San Francisco, where every U.S. President since Teddy Roosevelt has stayed when in the city, and The Plaza in New York. They also picked up a major challenge: what to name the hotels in this new evolution of the Brand?

A key driver behind CP's purchase of Fairmont was the fit between the iconic railway hotels of the former and the grand old U.S. properties of the latter. Even more important for CP, however, was securing a well-known Brand name that could be expanded throughout North America and around the world. The Canadian Pacific name simply didn't have the legs. For people outside of Canada, it conjured up images of railways (if anything at all), not luxury hotels.

Although its individual properties – like Quebec City's Chateau Frontenac and Alberta's Banff Springs Hotel – were endeared to locals and highly visible to high-end travelers worldwide, the CP Brand name itself was little-known. Thus the properties were not known by their Brand name – "CP Hotels" – but affectionately by their distinct local name – like the Royal York and Jasper Park Lodge. Because these local names were reservoirs of enormous Brand equity around the world, it would have been hugely wasteful to kill them off.

So what to call the hotels under the newly merged CP – Fairmont Brand? The decision was made to merge the Fairmont and CP local names together – as in "The Fairmont Banff Springs" and "The Fairmont Jasper Park Lodge."

It was a brilliant evolutionary move because people already attached to the properties could still use the local name. Residents of Toronto for example, still call their hotel "The Royal York." At the same time, foreign travelers

*It's what people think of you™

familiar with the Fairmont Brand – but not with the local names – will, in their minds, be staying at "The Fairmont" when they're visiting Toronto.

Atlas Air

While CP Hotels moved toward a new affiliation, Atlas Air ClimateCare moved away from one. Seventy-five years old at the time, Atlas Air belonged to a cooperative of companies, called ClimateCare, that specialized in HVAC (heating, ventilation and air conditioning). As the jewel in the ClimateCare crown, Atlas Air had expanded into a range of services beyond HVAC alone. And so it decided to part with ClimateCare and drop that part of its name.

We did a ThinkAudit to help them define a go-forward Brand strategy. Our interviews revealed a profoundly deep level of customer trust, built over many decades and based on their belief that Atlas Air employees truly cared.

And so *AtlasCare* became the logical, subtle name evolution for a Brand that was trying to move away from a past association, but not change so radically as to lose the Brand recognition accumulated over a span of eight decades.

Five People in a Room

Even if evolutionary, name changes are a temptation for old friend graphic designers who see it as an appropriate opportunity to make big changes to the logo, colors and other Brand identity elements. So we were not surprised when this urge came up at AtlasCare. Our coaching to the client was clear: the five of you in this room are ready to change your identity because you see it every day. You assume that your customers are as bored with it as you are. But your tens of thousands of customers only see it a few times a year on a handful of direct mail pieces. Change your appearance and they might not recognize you anymore.

And so it was that evolution, not revolution was applied not just to the name of this Brand, but to a refresh of its visual identity.

A Street Fight

As AtlasCare discovered, great success can bring Brand challenges with it. The success of KingStreet Capital Partners, Canada's leader in private equity real estate investments, led to a Brand challenge of the legal kind. KingStreet had not intended to enter the U.S. market, but did so on the strength of billions in deals over its first five years of existence.

*It's what people think of you™

Unfortunately, there was a New York firm with the same name who launched a costly trademark infringement challenge. And so our job was to rename the KingStreet organization.

At first, they wanted the name to be changed simply to initials – a common wish. But that approach was clearly not the right one in this case – because new clients would ask what the initials stood for, requiring that the story of the lawsuit be forever told.

 Our recommendation was to take an evolutionary approach that would preserve as much equity as possible from the KingStreet moniker. We went so far as to develop a new name and visual identity that sounded and looked similar to *KingStreet* – one that preserved the "word" and "shape" equity of that name.

The final choice was *KingSett Capital*. A "sett" being a small rectangular paving stone meant that even the legacy of Street was kept alive.

Evolution on the Fly

The air ambulance services for the Province of Ontario were faced with an evolutionary challenge created by a change in health care delivery. The provincial Ministry of Health had decided to combine its disparate air ambulance services into a single, coordinated unit.

The need to consolidate its fleet of helicopters and fixed-wing aircraft was severe. In a jurisdiction over one million kilometers square (bigger than Texas and Arizona combined), major hospitals had clustered themselves into "centers of excellence," making it more difficult to quickly, and under the highest level of care, transport acute and trauma patients to the specialized treatment they required.

Although people think of air ambulances as essentially a road ambulance with wings, the reality is extraordinary. They are virtual hospitals, staffed by elite paramedics who give care and receive training and equipment unheard of – even in the medical and emergency services community itself.

Thus we needed to evolve the Brand in a way that conveyed its 21st-century, cutting-edge expertise, while paying tribute to the important historic role it had served as an icon of hope and deliverance.

*It's what people think of you™

We were concerned that the term "air ambulance" did not properly reflect what these professionals actually did – so we introduced a new term: "transport medicine." We then extrapolated the orange details on their aircraft, painting all of their vehicles in that color and lending it to the new Brand name: *ornge*.

The identity of the evolved Brand is completed by a logo – which appears both as a pair of caring hands and a set of angel wings – that portrays two key Brand attributes. These unmistakable aircraft will have people cheering on ornge as they thunder overhead or land on hospital roofs, busy expressways and the evening news.

Betty Crocker

Evolution isn't always thrust upon you. It can be a continual thing done by design, as Betty Crocker has demonstrated with its regular updates to the iconic Betty character that adorns its baking product packaging.

This 85-year-old Brand evolves Betty's picture every few years, to keep her up-to-date and always representative of the target audience. In more recent iterations, the face has been a digitally-created combination of women's faces from different racial groups. I'm sure there have been 20 iterations over the years, keeping her fresh and of the moment (it's always been the hairstyles that especially date her). If you've known the Brand for years, you'd barely believe the picture has changed, the evolution is so smooth and well done.

Just Don't Do It

With old friends and new friends always lurking, resisting a revolutionary Brand overhaul is by no means easy. But consider what's at stake. Sweeping changes to an established Brand mean inconsistent messaging is reaching your stakeholders and especially your customers – the people out there who regard your Brand as "theirs." Customers, no longer sure what "their" Brand means, open their minds to competitive Brand messages – and one just might slip in and replace yours.

Brand: It ain't the logo*

*It's what people think of you™

[11] Branding is a Process, Not an Event

It takes time and persistence for your
Brand to sink in with stakeholders.
But losing hard-won Brand equity
can happen in the blink of an eye.
So pass on the Super Bowl approach
-- and stay focused on the long run.

"It takes 20 years to build a brand.
It takes 5 minutes to lose it."

Warren Buffet

Fast Food Nation. Super Size Me. Two powerfully influential movies to focus laser-like attention on the epidemic of obesity in North America and if, or to what extent, corporations should be held responsible for it in court. It's no small matter – a controversial 2005 study in the *New England Journal of Medicine* claimed that due to obesity, "youth of today may, on average, live less healthy and possibly even shorter lives than their parents[9]."

All over North America, boardrooms were sent squirming as the litigation heavyweights built their cases against fast food marketers. The big corporations who knew they were the likely targets were especially nervous and reacted early. Kraft, the marketer of Nabisco cookies, Oscar Meyer sliced meats, Philadelphia cream cheese and a multitude of other products, announced a set of "Global Initiatives To Help Address The Rise In Obesity." It reads like an accused criminal's desperate promise to reform.

The only thing harder than building a Brand is changing one that's established.

Be the Brand You Are

Yet the Kraft Brand was built brilliantly, by delivering consistent messages and experiences over many decades. Even with all of the negative press they've received, the bond they enjoy with their customers remains one of the world's strongest – because customers know what Kraft is.

It underlines the fact that a Brand must be true to itself. Lots of people drink alcohol, smoke cigarettes, buy gas-guzzling SUVs, lay in the sun – and even more people eat fatty foods, all by choice. They've all heard the risks and know the chances they are taking. What's more, Brands like Kraft and the many others that serve these markets make a lot of money.

Branding is a process, not an event. And the only thing harder than building a Brand is changing one that's established. So a Brand should think long and hard before trying to reposition itself. You will recall that TD realized they were a total pain to deal with, so they acquired customer-friendly Canada Trust in an effort to change perceptions. They now have a firm lock

*It's what people think of you™

on the "comfortable" position, but it took more than 10 years to do so – hardly an overnight success.

Fumbling the Brand

Branding isn't even an event at an event like the Super Bowl. Every year in the run-up to the NFL championship, there is more hype about the ads than there is about the game: cost per 30 seconds (approximately $3 million), who's in, who's out and stories about great ads of the past (like the 1984 Apple Computer ad, directed by no less than Ridley Scott – the Oscar-winning director of *Alien, Gladiator* and other Hollywood blockbusters).

While Super Bowl ads are wonderfully entertaining half-minute movies, they are not, for the most part, Brand builders – because all the excitement puts the participating companies under pressure to go off-Brand. The exorbitant, all-or-nothing cost has them questioning both their own sanity (should we be spending this much to send out the same old message?) and their strategy (surely this one-shot cost, in this high-creative environment, deserves something new and special!). And their creative partners, the guys who actually create these Super-commercials, are desperate to use this once-in-a-career opportunity to try something "revolutionary" to build their own reputations.

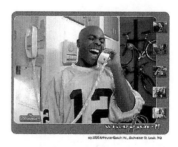

In a world where strong Brands are built with consistency of message and consistency over time, Super Bowl brings out the worst in Brand discipline – with negative results to match. The classic example is Budweiser's attention-getting "whassup?" campaign that launched at the Super Bowl in 2000 and led only to a sales drop. That year, Bud's market share decreased by between 1.5 and 2.5% and its sales of barrels fell by 8.3%[10]. Yet the campaign won the top prize at the advertisers' annual navel-gaze at Cannes. So the creatives obviously liked their own work, and the public got a good laugh from it, but at the end of the day, the target audience was left thinking, "Funny, but what's the King of Beers doing with the street-level whassup?"

Branding is Not an Event...

...But losing one often is. Just ask Toyota, whose massive recalls attracted more attention than a Super Bowl wardrobe malfunction.

In 2009, in the same week they passed General Motors as maker of the most cars on the planet, Toyota announced a first wave of recalls that would rock the Brand to its core. It had taken the Japanese automaker 50 years to achieve what they saw as the pinnacle of success: beating GM. Consumed with anticipation of that event, Toyota – absolutely legendary for its focus on quality – sped up the assembly line and lost its way.

The basis of the recalls was frightening both to consumers and the Brand: people were reporting that their Toyota vehicles were suddenly accelerating for no apparent reason. The story dominated the front pages for months. In the end, 9 million cars were recalled from every corner of the world.

No less than NASA was called in to conduct an investigation, which ultimately found that many cases of "unintended acceleration" were caused by driver error, but also by accelerator pedals stuck under floor mats and also by accelerator pedals that were just plain stuck.

Branding is not an event, but losing one often is. In the case of Toyota, this maxim applies on three levels. First, Toyota's focus on an event – passing GM in number of cars sold – made them abandon their longtime, consistent focus on a process that produced high-quality cars. Second were the recalls themselves, the most punishing events in the Brand's history. And finally, Toyota's GM obsession led to an event as unintended as sticking accelerators: the loss of a large portion of Brand equity.

Toyota's fixation on attaining scale larger than GM was foolishness. Compared to sticking with process and remaining the best-quality carmaker, that single event was of little worth to Toyota. Yet now they must stick with the process of regaining a quality-based Brand position in the eyes of consumers. And rebuilding is even tougher than building the Brand the first time.

Disconnected

Employees are essential to the success of that Brand-building process. While this may seem obvious, to many organizations it isn't.

*It's what people think of you™

Consider the story of Martin, a friend of co-author Andris Pone. Martin moved houses. Bell moved his phone line. But in its wisdom, Bell hooked up his service – Internet and all – to the credit card and debit terminal of an antique shop down the street.

Martin, who has a home-based business, was without service for five days. Using the landline of a neighbor, it took Martin almost seven hours with 310-BELL (Bell's helpdesk) to finally get service restored.

Yet Bell gave us reason to believe such a nightmare couldn't happen. I mean, shortly before Martin moved, they introduced a new logo. And a new tagline, *Today just got better*. And new advertising that featured iterations of the "er" in "better." Surely these initiatives should have prevented the upturning of Martin's life. Bell's new campaign was acclaimed, after all, as "a slick, bold and extraordinarily impressive brand strategy that uses a clean wordmark with a powerful voice."

But of course an ad campaign or a logo is not a Brand strategy at all.

Today just got better was supposed to be very much about Bell improving its often reprehensible customer service. If this new Brand promise was to be more than an empty shell, Bell's people obviously had to be coached on how to deliver it. Which a senior Bell VP seemed to appreciate, saying, "This is a significant rebrand from the basement up." Or as I would say, "Brands are built from the inside out."

"Good question: I have been asking too!"

Er...

Andris decided to test the VP's contention by calling three 310-BELL agents. Had Bell's front line people, frequently the only point of contact the company has with its many millions of customers, been coached on how to deliver *Today just got better*? Andris asked each agent what Bell's new ad campaign – "the one with the 'er's' in it," as he put it – meant. First call: "Good question: I have been asking too!" Second call: "I'd like to help you, but I'm in the billing department, so we don't know what the ads mean." Third call: "I haven't heard of it...I haven't watched TV lately."

It's what people think of you™

Clearly these crucial front line employees weren't given an ounce of training on their new "Brand." Bell had thought of their Brand evolution as an event – as rushing to market with an ad campaign – instead of as the more difficult but essential process of ensuring every employee first understood the new promise and how to deliver it.

Stay in Touch

One way to get the message out – inside and outside the organization – is with a regular blogpost distributed by email. Delivered on a ruthlessly consistent schedule, it's quite simply one of the most cost-effective ways to build your Brand.

Bringing in new business with it will of course be a process. Don't send out a single email and expect the phone to start ringing – that's just not going to happen. This is going to take time and commitment on your part. From our experience with our blog, entitled *instincts,* we know you have to send it out for a year or even more before you get much traction. It takes that long for people on your distribution list to request or refer your services – partly because they need to have confidence in you. That confidence comes from you being serious about sending out your publication on a regular basis.

instincts

Send it out to a list of clients, business associates, industry influencers, thought leaders and potential clients. We've sent out *instincts* every month for years (first as an e-newsletter), without fail. We're well over 100 issues and counting.

The purpose of the blog is primarily to stay top-of-mind with recipients. They may not read what we've written every time – but they at least see our email in their inbox and make a mental note that we're still working hard. Then someday – and this happens quite often – someone will suddenly need Branding assistance and we'll get a call, seemingly out of the blue. It might be from a person who's on our distribution list, or from someone who's received the blog as a forward from a friend.

The fact that the blogposts are getting forwarded hopefully indicates that they're an interesting, easily-digestible read demonstrating our firm's expertise and authority in the area of Brand. In your area of expertise, produce your blog to this same standard. Then know how much content to send out. Our view is that a blogpost should take 59 seconds or less to read.

Then there's the issue of frequency. Your blog must arrive on a regular, but not too frequent, basis – no more than once every two weeks. People's inboxes are full these days and you don't want to be part of the problem.

Remember:

Consistency is the number one rule of Branding. So whatever frequency and length you choose for your blog, the real art is to exercise the unfaltering discipline to get it done regularly and never, ever stop.

Branding for Dummies

The Super Bowl School of Branding introduces deadly inconsistency to your Brand. It also professes that Brands can be built in one fell swoop. Unfortunately, it takes more than 30 seconds to establish a relationship with stakeholders and earn their trust.

As tools of self-defense, Brands allow trusting stakeholders to ignore the marketing activities of other products and services and save mindshare for other, more important things. But when marketers change the message, they risk losing the attention and trust of stakeholders – and the stakeholders themselves.

While very, very few marketers will ever even come close to running an ad during the Super Bowl, they will all have moments of temptation. Temptation to do something out of their Brand's character for a special occasion. Temptation to say something different because their competitors are. Temptation to change what they stand for just because they're bored and assume everyone else is.

If you want your Brand to flourish, you've got to resist.

Brand: It ain't the logo*

*It's what people think of you™

[12] Deliver Great Experiences

Brand-Building Tool #3

Because every stakeholder interaction either adds to or detracts from your Brand, you've got to deliver at every touchpoint.

"[While the brand] promise can be brought to life in creative advertising and clever product placement, a brand can only truly be fulfilled if it is lived every day by the people behind the brand."

Carly Fiorina
Former CEO
Hewlett-Packard

Every time someone comes into contact with your Brand, one of two things happens.

1. Brand equity is created.
2. Brand equity is destroyed.

Your Brand has made certain promises to everyone who's aware of it. If the experiences people have with your Brand are consistent with those promises, Brand equity – defined as the retained, positive thoughts of stakeholders – gets a boost. If the experiences don't measure up, those positive thoughts deteriorate.

Brand "touchpoints" are the many situations in which all the people out there hope to experience your Brand promise. Organizations that use their Brand as a central operating principle and who have a Chief Brand Officer – vs. simply a CEO – use every single touchpoint to deliver an experience that reinforces the Brand.

The Starbucks Experience

One of the most consistent experiential Brands around is Starbucks, a massive global enterprise that's been built with considerable energy focused on what they call the Starbucks Experience. In North America, the Starbucks phenomenon has grown not with mass media advertising, but by turning customers into Brand evangelists. The converted tell their friends about the Starbucks experience, those friends wander into a store to check it out, and on it goes.

It's the baristas who make the coffee cool, more than any taste profile could ever do.

Go into a Starbucks and you'll see that delivering experiences is something they're passionate about. It's right in their lofty mission: *To inspire and nurture the human spirit – one person, one cup and one neighborhood at a time.*

The people that work at Starbucks are called "partners." Partners preparing the premium-priced coffee are called "baristas." In some respects the baristas are a varied group of individuals. They are mainly comprised of 20-something men and women. Although they represent many different ethnicities, it's easy to get the feeling that all baristas are alike. That's because they have some critical characteristics in common – characteristics that happen to be critical to properly and consistently delivering the Starbucks Experience. Baristas tend to be bright and well-educated: most are enrolled in post-secondary education and even graduate studies. They have a heightened sense of detail that comes in handy, no doubt, when trying to master the myriad beverage combinations on the menu. They are articulate in order to communicate effectively with their also well-educated customers. They're cool people hired and coached to treat customers like family.

Pre-Takeoff Tick Off

That's important because even a leader like Starbucks can sometimes stumble. I was at the airport for one of those ridiculous early morning check-ins and headed straight for my morning ritual – the Grande Bold – only to find people there who, to make a long story short, didn't give a damn about the Starbucks that legions of faithful customers know and love.

You see, many Starbucks stores are in fact not corporate-owned. While Starbucks doesn't franchise to individuals, they do form licensing arrangements with companies with desirable retail space – like the foodservice organizations that have airport contracts. At some of these stores, there can be factors outside of Starbucks' control, like unions, hiring, processes and training.

Obviously these are all vitally important to creating the Starbucks Experience. So these outlets struggle to replicate the Brand that loyal customers know and potential customers are looking for. Sure, the product in my airport coffee cup tasted about the same as usual, but a less than satisfactory experience drives home that  the coffee itself, while good, isn't really that different from what competitors offer. At Starbucks, it's the experience that differentiates the product.

Starbucks might want to reconsider its decision to introduce outlets in circumstances where it cannot ensure consistent provision of their full experience. Having locations in major airports is an obvious move because the demographics of air travelers fit a big chunk of the Starbucks customer profile: well-educated, high disposable income. But these locations can be just

*It's what people think of you™

as disastrous to the Brand if the experience is a letdown to new and existing customers alike.

Getting Burnt

The unsettling experience of Brand inconsistency, even at a runaway leader like Starbucks, recalls the "burnt" customers Michael E. Gerber refers to in his million-selling *The E-Myth Revisited: Why Most Small Businesses Don't Work And What To Do About It*[11]. Gerber recalls being delighted with the experience of his first haircut with a new barber:

> I went to a barber who, in our first meeting, gave me one of the best haircuts I had ever had. He was a master with the scissors and used them exclusively, never resorting to electric shears as so many others do. Before cutting my hair, he insisted on washing it, explaining that the washing made cutting easier. During the haircut, one of his assistants kept my cup of coffee fresh. In all, the experience was delightful, so I made an appointment to return.

> When I returned however, everything had changed. Instead of using the scissors exclusively, he used the shears about 50 percent of the time. He not only didn't wash my hair but never even mentioned it. The assistant did bring me a cup of coffee, but only once, never to return. Nonetheless, the haircut was excellent.

Gerber has a third cut, and the experience is different from both previous visits:

> As I left, something in me decided not to go back. It certainly wasn't the haircut – he did an excellent job. It wasn't the barber. He was pleasant, affable, seemed to know his business. It was something more essential than that.

> There was absolutely no consistency to the experience...What the barber did was to give me a delightful experience and then take it away.

Gerber ultimately connects these inconsistent experiences with the phenomenon in which children:

> are alternately punished and rewarded for the same kind of behavior. This form of behavior in a parent can be disastrous to the child; he never knows what to expect or how to act. It can also be disastrous to the customer... [the child], of course, has no choice but to stay with the parent. But the customer can go someplace else. And he will.

*It's what people think of you™

The *Ultimate Driving Experience* vs. *The Relentless Pursuit of Perfection*

BMW and Lexus are both highly experiential Brands. The rush of driving one of their fine automobiles is what it's all about – almost. Vitally important is the experience customers have after purchase, when they bring the car back to the dealer for service. The car is only  delivered once, but it's serviced about half a dozen times over the life of a typical lease – and the last service event is often just before the owner trades in the vehicle and considers whether to pick up the same Brand again.

At what point in this lifecycle do you think the dealer should be focusing most intensely on ensuring positive customer experiences? Answer: at every point.

Let me share with you a friend's experience with his new BMW 645 that seriously impressed him – and then let him down in a big way. He went to pick up his vehicle in the dealer's beautiful, transparent glass tower through which commuters on the adjacent highway can see all the different models on display, stacked up like so many toy cars. Delivery actually took place on the 4th floor of the tower! After a complete personal briefing on every aspect of running the car, he and his new Beemer were whisked down to street level in a car elevator – a very cool start indeed to the new relationship.

Now fast forward to the first time the car required service. The same BMW dealer has only one young woman you can speak with to arrange your service appointment. Nice touch. Having just one person dedicated to these customer interactions should be a terrific way to personalize relationships – if you don't have to play endless phone tag with her, as my friend had to.

When the service appointment is finally made, my friend arrives early in the morning. No priority system for speaking with the service agents on duty is in evidence, so customers must jostle uncomfortably for position. When check-in is finally complete and it's time for a courtesy ride to work, everyone must wait until a large enough group assembles to be loaded into a minivan that is decidedly not BMW. Then, in the uncomfortable silence of strangers, the group is shuttled into the city and dropped off school bus style. For these busy customers – who are anything but cost sensitive – this isn't exactly the ultimate service experience they were expecting from BMW ownership.

Contrast that experience with the one I enjoy as a Lexus customer. I call the special Lexus service number and make an appointment the first time I call, every time. When I arrive for my appointment, I drive right into the dealer's building and stop outside the private office of the Service Manager, who opens my door for me, greets me by name and invites me into his office while he personally retrieves my mileage. Details obtained, he hands me his business card and invites me to visit the Hertz counter right across from his office, *right in the dealership*, where they give me a fresh new Lexus to experience for the day.

Question:

Which would you call "The Ultimate Service Experience"?

On top of that remark-able service experience, I receive a magazine exclusively for Lexus owners. It all goes to show that Lexus clearly understands that the Brand experience is about a lot more than just the buying process or the automobile itself. They've modeled the after-purchase experience on the overall promise of the Brand as epitomized by their positioning statement: *The relentless pursuit of perfection.* They've made the after-sales relationship a luxury experience in which the comfort and satisfaction of the driver is paramount and everything works as it should, just like in the car itself.

BMW needs to recreate its service experience by aligning it with the ambitious promise of *The ultimate driving experience.* Here's an idea: instead of the boring minivan, they can use employee graduates from their own BMW Driver Training program to whisk BMW owners to work in the latest demos – ensuring the ultimate driving experience continues throughout the ownership timeline.

Even a Box Can Be an Experience

I love telling the story of one particular visit to DMD, the very successful retail design company owned by designer David Milne. DMD has created customer experiences for a diverse range of clients including Loblaws, Nike and Victoria's Secret. During my tour, David inspired me with a little sidebar about Apple computers:

I always insist that my staff wait for me to open any box with new product we buy from Apple. I just love their packages. Every graphic, every packing piece is

*It's what people think of you™

> beautiful and well thought out. Everything fits and is presented as a piece of art. Even their Styrofoam is beautiful! And finally, when you unwrap the computer itself, it is beautiful. The whole thing is a wonderful experience.

That's for sure. On YouTube there are people who've actually filmed themselves opening an Apple product, zooming in on every last detail of unwrapping their new toy.

Think about the remark-able consistency of the package-opening experience with other Apple touchpoints. There is the friendliness of the products, and the One to One sessions during which you learn about your Apple product. There is the straightforward layout of the Apple Store – and the fact that while you're there you can actually use the devices and create something on the spot. And when you are ready to pay, don't look for the cash register: they have been replaced by wireless payment systems that come to you.

Need some proof that the effort of ensuring a consistently on-Brand experience is worth it? How about this: the average Apple Store has a relative handful of items for sale in just a few thousand square-feet of real estate. The average Home Depot has hundreds of thousands of SKUs and over a hundred thousand square feet. And the Apple Store outsells the Home Depot $43 million to $30 million per year per store.

Enough said.

The Apple Store outsells the Home Depot $43 million to $30 million per year, per store.

The Briefcase

Had I asked him, I expect David would have had a similar opinion of Steam Whistle Brewing, another company that looks at its products from an experiential point of view. This premium-priced microbrewery beer has been built through careful attention to detail that reinforces its retro-quality position. The 12-packs are a handsome presentation with a surprisingly comfortable briefcase handle that actually works and feels solid in the hand. The case recloses snugly, so it's easy to store or return for the bottle deposit refund.

*It's what people think of you™

The bottles, which are 30% heavier than the industry norm, feel substantial. The graphics are beautiful raised-letter printing right on the glass. The closure is the old style pry-off cap that presents a rounded, soft-on-the-mouth opening. The beer tastes good. I've done a ThinkAudit with their customers, and they talk about the quality of Steam Whistle unaided. They defend the premium price as understandable and worth it.

Of course, the experience you create for your stakeholders does not have to be as lovely as what Apple or Steam Whistle might craft. Flimsy packaging is just fine if you are selling a non-premium product. It's all about being true to your Brand, whatever that Brand may be.

Consider Budweiser, a bona fide working man's Brand and one of the top-selling beers in the world. Compared to Steam Whistle, their cases are a demonstration in production minimalism – thin, wobbly, cheap (never try to pick one up after it's been opened). The bottle is the industry standard with the screw-off cap, which is exactly how it feels on your mouth. The label is a randomly stuck-on paper thing. It all comes across as blue collar – and Bud's busy bean counters will confirm that there's absolutely nothing wrong with that.

Brand Theater

Another aspect of the Steam Whistle experience is their brewery tours. Their production facilities are situated in The Roundhouse, an historic building that was once a repair station for steam locomotives. Roundhouse visitors can take the Souvenir Tour, the Six Pack Tour or the Twelve Pack Tour. Getting people to touch and taste the product, understand the history, meet the people behind it and visit the place where it's made builds an emotional bond with customers, setting Steam Whistle apart and helping to establish long-term Brand loyalty.

Crayola, that most colorful of children's craft companies, takes a similar approach at its head office and manufacturing facility in Easton, Pennsylvania. They offer very special experiences at the Crayola Factory Hands-on Discovery Center, where kids and their parents can learn about Crayola's history, buy their

*It's what people think of you™

favorite crayon colors by the pound, try and test all the Crayola products in specialized test labs and experiment with new marker technology.

It's brilliant Brand theater. I know a mother of two who visited the Factory and spent two busy hours there. She returned home with a new mindset – to never again purchase discounted coloring products. From now on, only Crayola will do.

Proverbs and Toilet Paper

Procter & Gamble's Charmin toilet paper used to run a highly original piece of Brand theater with an 18-wheeled "Potty Palooza," dedicated to "saving people from the unbearable portalet." The Palooza toured 30 venues annually throughout the United States – everything from the Super Bowl to the Arizona Balloon Festival – with one of the world's largest sampling programs. Each year, it got five million people to sample Charmin's key attribute – softness.

The 27 bathrooms on wheels were a shiny, clean oasis in the often unkempt world of fairs and sporting event restrooms – the perfect stop to build a positive relationship with a Charmin experience. In the words of Charmin, the restrooms are "adorned with all the amenities you would find at home – from wallpaper and skylights to hardwood floors and televisions. And, of course, there's always plenty of Charmin Ultra." At one venue, 30,000 people signed a petition to get the Palooza to return the following year!

In a sign of the times, the Potty Palooza has been replaced with a new experience: an iPhone application called "SitOrSquat," that helps consumers find the cleanest public toilets worldwide. The application and supporting website offer user-generated listings of bathroom locations and ratings, as well as details on hours of operation, handicap accessibility, showers and availability of changing tables.

There is Only One Strategy

Trying to reach out with traditional marketing methods like trade publications, direct mail, cold-calling or TV ads has never been more expensive or less effective. And when you realize that ultimately there are no products and no services – just experiences – you realize that experience delivery is the only enduring strategy.

Brand: It ain't the logo*

*It's what people think of you™

[13] Make the Story Live and Breathe

Strong Brands are profoundly
rich with elements that cannot be
captured in a single Brand Foundation.
But these attributes are every bit as
vital to the Brand's sense of identity.

"Living out the brand promise doesn't
come solely from mission statements.
Or product differentiation. Or snappy logos.
It flows from the intersection of culture and
people. It flows from the living, breathing
brand."

Jim Kelly
Former Chairman
UPS

Great Brands have a clear sense of who they are because the original core purpose, vision, mission, position and other key Brand components are constantly top of mind for everyone in the organization. Not every business will call it a "foundation" per se – but almost without exception, the strongest Brands adhere to foundational elements that are passed down through generations of management and employees. These elements are easily referred to as a guide in decision after decision, year after year, good times and bad.

A Single, Common Reference Point

In this way, the Brand becomes institutionalized – formally ingrained in the organization as the common thread running through the culture even as people (Brand leaders like the CBO especially) come and go. It allows the Brand to be "lived" – to be referred to as a single, common reference point to guide every decision, every day, by everyone.

The point of institutionalizing the Brand throughout the organization is to make the Brand live and breathe for those responsible for it – meaning you and everyone else where you work. The Brand needs to live and breathe so you can convey a consistent Brand to your stakeholders – so they maintain a rock-solid impression of what value they get from you and accordingly, stay engaged.

Jim Casey

United Parcel Service has almost 400,000 employees, delivers to 220 countries and owns 60% of the ground shipping business in the United States. It's been more than 50 years since Jim Casey, the man who founded UPS in 1907, retired as CEO. In Casey's era, the company was entirely owned by employees, and it's predominantly worker-owned today. Yet these people are still heard to say: "This is Jim Casey's company[12]."

Why? Because Casey held dear a set of crucial Brand values and was masterful at giving them life within his company. He defined service as "the sum of many little things done well." And to this day, work practices at UPS are subject to constant scrutiny, revision and immaculate documentation. Consider the time-saving mandates of the Standard Practice Manual, which requires that delivery drivers hold their keychains on their pinky fingers to avoid fumbling with keys. It also specifies that seatbelts be inserted with the left hand, so the ignition can be simultaneously started with the right.

*It's what people think of you™

10%

From Casey's perspective, the single most important contributor to the success of UPS was employee ownership. So when UPS needed money for acquisitions in 1999, 16 years after Casey's death, CEO Jim Kelly agonized "over whether we could go public and maintain our corporate culture. If we couldn't reconcile the two, we wouldn't have done it." In light of their culture, how much ownership of the company did UPS ultimately sell to the public? Just 10%. Employees still control the stock through shares that have 10 times the voting rights as those issued to the public at large.

15%

To the extent that employee ownership and attention to detail are Brand hallmarks of UPS, entrepreneurship and innovation rule at 3M. This is a company with a very canny knack for developing products that reach generic status: that is, their Brand names – like Scotch Tape, Scotch Guard and Post-It Notes – become the monikers for entire categories.

At 3M, innovative behavior is hard-wired into work processes and even compensation. Their "15% Rule" demands that all 3M engineers spend 15% of their time working on what- ever projects they like[13]. The initiative isn't something cooked up as the latest management fad, far from it. William McKnight, CEO from 1929 to 1966, implemented the 15% Rule and is credited as the man responsible for ingraining 3M's entrepreneurial culture. "If you put fences around people, you get sheep" he would say. Internet-age companies have taken note. In an apparent nod to 3M, Google has a 20% rule.

30%

Long after McKnight's departure came the 30% Rule – that each company division must generate at least 30% of its sales from products introduced in the current year.

These cultural artifacts are serious business at 3M. They're not something you tinker with – something James McNerney, the very first 3M CEO who came from outside the internal ranks, understands: "I think we're world class at the front end of the [innovation] process. If I dampen our enthusiasm for that, I've really screwed it up."

How Many Blades?

Gillette is another organization that's maintained amazing Brand consistency over a very long period of time. Their claim to fame is the way they introduce razors that make their own models obsolete. Their current top razor, the Fusion ProGlide Power, will probably not be by the time you read this sentence.

Where does this burning need to innovate come from? Try 1921. A number of the company's patents were set to expire that year. Anticipating a deluge of knockoffs, the company's founder, King Camp Gillette, introduced a new razor and promoted it by criticizing its predecessor with ads reading "Any razor you've ever known is crude[14]."

The Brand still doesn't wait for rivals. Like Intel with its computer chips, Gillette stands for the very latest in performance and quality. For more than 80 years of rock-solid Brand consistency, Gillette gets to sell five times more razors than its nearest "competitor."

"I think we're world class at the front end of the [innovation] process. If I dampen our enthusiasm for that, I've really screwed it up."

We Are Not in Business to Make Profits

Johnson & Johnson, founded in 1886, is the company that brought us the original First Aid Kit and the Band-Aid, among many other legendary Brands. Robert Wood Johnson II, son of the company founder, defined the company's philosophy early on by saying "We are not in business to make profits; we are in business to earn them by serving our customers[15]." In 1943 he formalized these beliefs into a detailed statement of responsibilities, called the Credo, that's been the basis of their Brand ever since.

Killer Headaches

The Credo is posted at every Johnson & Johnson facility around the world and is carved in an eight-foot-high piece of limestone at the company headquarters in New Jersey. But don't think for a minute that the Credo is just

*It's what people think of you™

an empty exercise in corporate PR. The Credo details the company's responsibilities, as it sees them, to four stakeholder groups: customers, employees, communities and shareholders. For example:

> We believe our first responsibility is to the doctors, nurses and patients, to mothers and fathers and all others who use our products and services.

And later:

> We are responsible to the communities in which we live and work and to the world community as well. We must be good citizens, support good works and charities and bear our fair share of taxes.

It is the Credo's delicate balance of stakeholders' sometimes contradictory interests that company executives cite as helping Johnson & Johnson survive the "Tylenol Crises." In 1982, seven people in the United States died after ingesting cyanide-laced Tylenol. The company was expected to meet a similar fate. But Johnson & Johnson inspired public trust by honest and open disclosure, quick removal of product from the shelves and by taking a $100 million charge against earnings. Another person died when a second tampering crisis hit in 1986. The product was discontinued but eventually reintroduced with tamper-evident packaging.

In time, Johnson & Johnson's principled handling of these episodes earned them back all of the market share they had lost.

Profit

Southwest Airlines, founded in 1971, has a Brand as deep-rooted and distinct as their absolutely exceptional record for customer service and profitability. The Brand is all about having fun, treating co-workers and customers like family, and very hard work. In an industry notorious for shoddy service, Southwest has received the fewest customer complaints of any major U.S. carrier every year since 1987.

And they've made a profit 38 years running. This when most of the other major U.S. airlines have been in and out of bankruptcy. In the aftermath of September 11, 2001, the other airlines laid off 120,000 workers. Southwest? Zero. Not one. And they *still* made a profit.

It's what people think of you™

As the company grew rapidly in the 1990s, senior management realized that its many new hires didn't have the perspective on the company that its veteran employees did[16]. They didn't know all the stories that collectively defined the history of Southwest's fun and family focus. As long-time employees grew older and near retirement, company leaders were afraid their knowledge would be lost to future generations.

The Rocking Chair Sessions

And so the "rocking chair sessions" were born. Held regularly in departmental meetings throughout the company, veteran and soon-to-retire employees would literally sit in a rocking chair in front of the group and talk about "the old days." The rocking chair sessions were an instant hit and became a regular agenda item.

Googol

"Google" is certainly one of the odder and more memorable Brand names ever coined. Many people view it as a nonsensical name, cooked up entirely because it's easy to recall.

But no. It was the savvy and deliberate choice of founders Larry Page and Sergey Brin to institutionalize the company's mission: *To organize the world's information and make it universally accessible and useful.* Google's name is a play on the word "googol," defined as a number represented by the numeral 1 followed by 100 zeros. As Google puts it on their website, "use of the term reflects the company's mission to organize the immense, seemingly infinite amount of information available on the web."

Googleplex

That's one ambitious mission. And with the prodigious rate at which technology advances and competition moves, it's not something that's going to be pulled off by two guys locked alone in a room. Together with big brains and lots of money, it's going to require exceptionally close teamwork and lightning speed. Hence the layout of the Googleplex, the firm's headquarters in Santa Clara County, California.

Every aspect of the Googleplex is designed to be flexible for the purpose of accelerating the exchange of ideas. Large rubber exercise balls, easily moved from one area to another, are used as office chairs. There are no cubicle walls. Desks in the early days (i.e. around 2000), were wooden doors held up by pairs of sawhorses. Founders Larry and Sergey led weekly "TGIF" meetings in the open space among the desks.

Google found that the atmosphere breeds "both collegiality and an accelerated exchange of ideas":

> Ideas are traded, tested and put into practice with an alacrity that can be dizzying. Meetings that would take hours elsewhere are frequently little more than a conversation in line for lunch and few walls separate those who write the code from those who write the checks. This highly communicative environment fosters a productivity and camaraderie fueled by the realization that millions of people rely on Google results. Give the proper tools to a group of people who like to make a difference, and they will[17].

Veteran companies like UPS, 3M and Gillette show us that Brands can retain their meaning for a phenomenally long time – long after their founders have moved on or died – but that it doesn't just happen by magic. To last, the Brand must be formalized and relentlessly permeated throughout and beyond the organization in a deliberate manner.

Everyone's Responsibility

Getting everyone to understand the importance of walking your Brand talk, to do it and say it the same way every day, is the best way to ensure you can deliver on your Brand promise in the long term. This means making everyone responsible for living the Brand. Not just the marketing department, but everyone – from shipping to engineering to finance. Everyone.

The Brand resides in sweeping initiatives like the 30% Rule and in details that to some seem mundane. But if you want your Brand position to be that of innovation leader in your industry, you can't be seen to still hand-write checks, have a lame website or not understand e-commerce. You'd better be offering your employees direct deposits, ordering from suppliers online, embracing mobile and featuring video streaming on your website. If you're not, your market-facing promise of innovation won't be believed by stakeholders either outside or inside your firm.

*It's what people think of you™

The gap between what you say you are and what people think you are breeds doubt in stakeholder minds. And that's a bad thing, because in this hyper-competitive world, the next Brand is just waiting for a moment of un-certainty to slip in and grab the mindshare formerly devoted to you.

[14]   Be the Mythographer

Although it's vital that formal
Brand components be conveyed
verbally and in print, they can only
achieve full clarity and viral power
when ingrained in stories.

"The story – from Rumpelstiltskin to
War and Peace – is one of the basic tools
invented by the human mind for the purpose
of understanding. There have been great
societies that did not use the wheel, but
there have been no societies that did
not tell stories."

Ursula K. Le Guin

There is a well-known story within Canada's largest privately-owned printing company, St. Joseph's Corporation. It is said that the founder literally walked out of a lucrative deal with a potential partner when he realized they printed Penthouse magazine. For the founder of St. Joseph's, a partnership arrangement with such a company was at odds with his personal morality.

At Nordion, a health and sciences company, employees recount with tearful pride how their leaders walked the talk of one of their stated values – *Genuine concern and respect for people* – and sent a major financial donation to the American Red Cross on the very afternoon of the 9/11 tragedy.

Formal Brand Components

We've seen how the Credo at Johnson & Johnson is cited 60 years later to guide decisions within the Brand. We've seen how the Standard Practice Manual gives UPS workers the highly detailed guidance essential to success in the regimented world of courier services. And we've seen how the 15% and 30% rules at 3M have institutionalized their innovation and entrepreneurial position – key to the Brand's success since its founding over a century ago.

Those are formal pieces of a Brand's foundational components. They appear on wall-mounted plaques, within policy documents and in the case of Johnson & Johnson, carved within an eight-foot chunk of rock. They are believed and lived by the company leadership of these world-leading organizations and relentlessly communicated throughout. Internally, they impart a strong sense of purpose and camaraderie that keeps the business focused on achieving its vision. In turn, a sharp internal focus builds ever more confidence and commitment in external stakeholders, who receive a stream of consistent and expected experiences with the Brand.

But all of the well-intentioned printing, framing and verbal recounting of formal Brand components – be they corporate values, vision statements, quality measurements, whatever – won't have the same clarity, viral potential or power of those ingrained in stories.

Stories Are Better Than Facts

As Daniel H. Pink writes in his fascinating book, *A Whole New Mind*, stories are easier to recall than facts: "Stories are easier to remember – because in many ways, stories are how we remember[18]." A list of corporate values is a list of facts. A mission statement is a statement of facts. But in an age of hyper-messaging, when we have an infinite number of facts at our fingertips, facts risk losing their power: "What begins to matter more is the ability to place these facts in context and to deliver them with emotional impact[19]."

By Telling Stories

Pink borrows from the observation of E.M. Forster to tell us that "a fact is 'the queen died and the king died.' A story is 'the queen died and the king died of a broken heart[20].'"

Some very big organizations understand the power of stories[21]. At 3M, top executives get storytelling lessons. Knowledge management programs at NASA use storytelling. Xerox realized that its repair people learn about fixing different machines by swapping stories with their colleagues – not by reading repair manuals. So the company organized these stories into a database, called Eureka, estimated by Fortune magazine to be worth $100 million.

Organizational storytelling has even spawned a new industry. StoryQuest is a Chicago business that will send interviewers to your firm, record the stories your people tell and then produce CDs that communicate your culture back to you. In the U.K., Richard Olivier, son of Laurence Olivier, has clients act out the plays of Shakespeare to bring forth lessons on leadership and governance.

Be the Mythographer

Beginning with the CBO, organizational leaders have a responsibility to communicate formal Brand components up and down the enterprise. Equally, it is incumbent upon them to be mythographers – to seek out, sculpt and tell the Brand's stories with purpose, pride and humility.

Kinds of Stories

Compelling Brand stories act as positive reinforcement of the Brand's position. Along the way they also speak to one or more elements of the Brand Foundation.

Stories about Going Above and Beyond

Luxury hotel companies are especially rich with stories that celebrate their Brands. The informal history of Four Seasons, for example, overflows with anecdotes of employees going above and beyond for their guests. Including the one about the doorman who, using his own funds and without asking for permission, followed a guest by plane to return a forgotten briefcase in time for an important meeting.

Kyu Lee, CEO of QUEUE, encourages employees to tell stories about how they or their colleagues have lived the Brand position of *Extraordinary service experiences*. Like the story of the technician who, on his own initiative, spent four hours in a cab to spend five minutes fixing the crucial connectivity issue of a grateful customer.

It is incumbent upon organizational leaders to be mythographers – to seek out, sculpt and tell the Brand's stories with purpose, pride and humility.

Stories that Customers Tell Each Other

Adding to anecdotes such as these are the countless stories that Four Seasons' guests tell others about a remark-able stay. Four Seasons manages beautiful properties, absolutely, but just ask anyone who's stayed at one of their hotels what made it so great. Chances are they won't talk about the room or the facilities. Instead they'll tell you a story about how wonderful the service was, including employees who somehow know and remember your name.

Stories about Famous Customers

Stories about hotel Brands don't always relate to going above and beyond. Serving to sweeten the appeal of the Brand to the more typical travelers among us, many stories talk about esteemed Brand patrons.

Ritz-Carlton, recognized within the hotel industry as Four Seasons' closest rival in the luxury category, is one of only five companies in the United States to win the Malcolm Baldrige National Quality Award on two occasions.

That's a more recent part of its story, which dates to the Brand's namesake, Cesar Ritz, dubbed "the king of hoteliers and the hotelier of kings" in early 20th-century Europe. The Brand also proudly tells of iconic guests including Howard Hughes, Irving Berlin and Bette Davis. These are stories that build pride both inside and outside the organization – cementing employees' choice to work there and guests' decision to stay.

Stories about Important Products

Stories can also describe the origins of particular products that are especially important to the Brand. Now a key part of the lore at Westin Hotels & Resorts, for example, is the origin of its much-celebrated Heavenly Bed. It was Barry Sternlicht, Chairman and CEO of parent Starwood at the time, who based the Bed and its linens on his own bed at home.

Stories about a Brand's Beginnings

Many stories recall how events early in the life of a Brand acted to shape its identity from that point forward. Communicating the heritage and premium-quality attributes of the Sleeman Breweries Brand is the story of how the founder of the present-day entity got into the business through a seemingly incredible coincidence. In 1984, just when John Sleeman was developing an interest in the beer brewing trade, an aunt handed him a leather-bound book of recipes used by John's great-great-grandfather. Until that moment, John apparently had no idea that beer was part of the family legacy.

As it turns out, another ancestor, George A. Sleeman, was caught smuggling beer over the U.S. border to Detroit in the Prohibition era – perhaps accounting for the family's silence on the issue to little John.

Stories about Traumatic Events

Shaping the identity of Johnson & Johnson was the devastating San Francisco earthquake of 1906. The company was the single largest donor of relief supplies to the city and cancelled all invoices of $100 ($15,000 in today's equivalent) or less. It was a show of corporate responsibility that permanently set the foundation for the company's behavior and most tangibly, for its 1943 Credo.

On a less traumatic note, ever wonder where William McKnight of 3M got the 15% idea? Probably from his own mistakes. McKnight, the driving force behind the culture of innovation and entrepreneurship at 3M, was highly tolerant of the errors implicit in experimentation because he famously made so many mistakes of his own.

Michael Dell Dropped Out

With a net worth in the many billions, Michael Dell is founder of the Brand that, second only to HP, manufactures the most personal computers in the world. The mass-customization model he pioneered allows customers to self-order a computer tailored to their specific desires.

Dell began his career selling PCs from his dorm room as a student at the University of Texas at Austin. At the age of 19, he was making $80,000 a month – just enough dough, apparently, to justify dropping out.

I can't be sure that Dell would suggest anyone follow the same route he did. But the story of his abbreviated college career is a key part of the Dell company legend because it epitomizes the brilliance of his Brand's people and their drive to meet customer needs.

So Did Bill Gates

In fact, among the titans of the personal computer and Internet age, Michael Dell's decision to quit college is strikingly common. Joining him on the dropout list are Bill Gates and the co-founders of Apple, Steve Jobs and Steve Wozniak. Clearly these individuals did not need a post-secondary education to help them get ahead. They have revolutionized multiple industries, and in the process, facilitated the creation of inestimable wealth.

Yet the fact that each man is a college dropout remains a key piece of his Brand's mythology. These stories contribute to Brand equity because they underline exactly how brilliant these men are. And their brilliance manifests as a halo effect around the whole company, validating customers' buy decisions both before and after purchase.

Mythology Can Get Hard-Wired

A piece of the Amazon story demonstrates how Brand mythology can, over time, transition from oral history into a part of day-to-day operations just as

*It's what people think of you™

formalized as a mission statement on a wall. Amazon.com launched in 1995 and year after year, lost up to hundreds of millions of dollars. The company didn't turn an annual profit until 2003.

In the midst of the losses, Amazon founder Jeff Bezos wanted to set an example of frugality. Along with driving a Honda (even though his personal worth was $500 million on paper), he worked on a desk that was actually a door. The legs of the "Door Desk" were two-by-fours, attached to the door by metal brackets.

That's the mythology. But frugality has turned into a formalized part of Amazon because, even though the Brand is now posting profits in the billions, Bezos and his employees still use Door Desks in a demonstration of their commitment to keeping costs down.

Amazon, Hewlett-Packard, Apple and Google all started in the garage.

Garage Brands

Another strand of Amazon's frugality story is that Bezos started his business in a garage. It turns out that Hewlett-Packard, Apple and Google all started in garages too – humble beginnings that live on in the hearts, minds and actions of all who work for these world-class companies.

The story of HP's beginnings holds an especially important place in the consciousness of that company and indeed, the whole of Silicon Valley. In 1939, William Hewlett and David Packard launched their company in a Palo Alto, California, garage. Lit by a single light bulb, it is considered Silicon Valley's birthplace, the spot where Hewlett and Packard worked through the 1950s to build equipment like oscillators and atomic clocks.

The garage is the physical manifestation of HP employees' intense pride in their origins. In 1999, then-CEO Carly Fiorina revitalized the Brand around it, introducing the "Rules of the Garage," a list of 10 dictums crystallizing the innovative bent of the HP founders. For example: "Perform more than you promised. If the person at the next bench sees what you're working on and doesn't say, 'Wow!' start over."

*It's what people think of you™

Then Fiorina had a replica of the original garage (which still existed but which HP no longer owned) reproduced on the company's corporate grounds. An ad campaign followed in which Carly declared: "The company of Bill Hewlett and Dave Packard is being reinvented. The original startup will act like one again. Watch!"

Tell Me a Story

Tell Brand stories at every opportunity. Illustrate your corporate values in action by retelling the company's founding whenever someone new joins the team. In an email to everyone at the beginning of each week, tell stories of customer service success. Before you know it, your customers will be telling them too.

[15] Great Names Mean Business

Brand naming is one of the most cost-effective – and underused – opportunities to tell your story and connect with stakeholders.

"Given several hundred million dollars and the ability to sustain heavy levels of spending behind a brand, you can make a generic, descriptive, uninteresting name stand for something and sell at the shelf – sometimes."

Carol L. Bernick
Chairman
Alberto-Culver

What's a *Zoosk*?

It's a Brand that wasted millions on advertising because its name is meaningless. It's possible that because of that advertising, you know that Zoosk is a dating website. But decide for yourself: if you ran a dating site and wanted to get the most bang for your communications buck, would you want a name like *Zoosk*, or would you prefer *Match, eHarmony* or *Plenty of Fish* – names that hint strongly at what these Brands are, what value they offer and how they are different from competitors?

Great names mean business – and names like *Zoosk* just don't do the job. Or rather, the jobs:

1. Be remark-able
2. Communicate the Brand Foundation
3. Integrate with the positioning statement
4. Be distinct
5. Be memorable
6. Inspire and attract stakeholders
7. Leverage an existing naming system, or create a new one
8. Be workable into a suitable domain name
9. Pass linguistics
10. Pass legal

As we'll see, this is a very tough list to fulfill.

Job 1: Be Remark-Able

Great names boost your bottom line by being remark-able. In our crazy world of hyper-messaging and hyper-choice, they make it easy for people – potential and actual employees, customers and all stakeholders – to understand who you are and what you're offering. They make it easy for people to decide if they want to buy in or opt out, and for your advocates to tell the story to others. They are deep reservoirs of meaning that you can access for telling your story now, and long into the future as you write new chapters.

Word-of-mouth being less expensive and more effective than paid communications, great names are one of the most cost-effective methods of communicating value.

Your Feelings

A quick word about your feelings: they don't matter. That's the sometimes very challenging reality you must accept when naming a Brand. It doesn't matter what you're naming – an organization, product, service, program, business unit or anything else – the question is not whether you subjectively "like" or "love" a potential name. You have to be objective – because for many reasons, you must be willing to accept a name other than your first choice. In our overcommunicated world, the relevant question is whether the name does the jobs – thereby cutting expenses and driving revenue.

Job 2: Communicate the Brand Foundation

Before you can name something, you have to know what it is. Which means building a Brand Foundation for it. If you try to name your Brand without first knowing what it is – without knowing what you are trying to describe – you will end up slapping together a partial Brand Foundation on the fly. With an incomplete understanding of your Brand, there's a very good chance you'll end up creating a *Zoosk* that fails to tell your story.

Before you can name something, you have to know what it is.

Telling stories is of course the single most effective way to communicate a Brand's meaning. Compose your Brand Foundation with wording that sets up stakeholders to tell your stories with ease. Then, using your Foundation's language to brainstorm, arrive at a Brand name with exactly the same storytelling potential. Your new, remark-able name will allow people to quickly get a sense of your Brand and be in a position to tell others about it.

Crumb-y

Dan Hoffman and Chris Borowski decided to open an upscale café-restaurant in Toronto that featured fresh-made-daily gelato. The name they were going to pick was *Cones*, inspired by the New York bakery *Crumbs*. But wait: what made Chris and Dan's venture different and highly remark-able was their combined 50 years of work experience at luxury hotel Brands including Hyatt and Four Seasons. *Cones* said absolutely nothing about that. Any customer conversations about the name (there would not have been many) would have quickly hit a dead end – without reference to the café's origins in fine hotels and the expectation that the Cones experience would live up to that pedigree.

Value of the *Cones* name to the bottom line? Absolute zero.

Dan and Chris were easily convinced that the best name for their venture was in fact *Hotel Gelato*, with the positioning statement *Stay for dessert.* An especially exciting benefit of the name was the potential it unleashed for the venue's theme and décor. Dan and Chris had no plans for their café to evoke a stylish boutique hotel until the Hotel Gelato name was presented to them. Now the place has funky chandeliers, banquettes and clocks showing not the times at international capitals, but at some of the world's most promi-

nent hotels. The bustling café has attracted a loyal group of customers and even an internationally-covered celebrity drop-in from Tom Cruise and daughter Suri.

Hotel Gelato demonstrates that Foundation-based, remark-able names don't just inspire opportunities to perpetuate the Brand through storytelling, but also drive alignment of every aspect of the Brand experience.

Just What You Need

The Brand name need not reference every element of the Brand Foundation. You will find that some elements – the position, for example, as with Hotel Gelato – provide more fodder for naming than others. As was the case with the value Brand of Canadian Tire – Canada's largest retailer, with annual sales in the range of $10 billion. The company's executive leadership gave us a ring after reading this book's first edition.

Unlike several competitors, including Walmart, Canadian Tire did not have its own value Brand. So it sought an in-house label to apply across a wide range of product categories. The Brand position was that it would offer similar quality to the competitive national Brands but at a lower price, and with fewer "bells and whistles."

*It's what people think of you™

After considering hundreds of names and dozens of positioning statements, *LikeWise* was the choice that expressed the position most clearly, by conveying the value Brand's "like," but not identical, qualities when compared to the national Brands. The chosen positioning statement – *Just what you need* – reinforced the fewer-bells-and-whistles aspect of the position, and through a double entendre, tells consumers that LikeWise is exactly what they need. The name has been rolled out to hundreds of products and could eventually adorn everything from spark plugs to lawn furniture.

Job 3: Integrate with the Positioning Statement

Notice that with *Hotel Gelato* and *LikeWise*, the positioning statements capitalize on the opportunity to continue the story told by the name. *Stay for dessert* uses layers of meaning to enhance both the "hotel" and "gelato" aspects of *Hotel Gelato*. *Just what you need* reinforces the "like" but not identical features of the national Brand.

Then consider the name *BlackBerry*. It opens up all kinds of opportunities, which BlackBerry has mostly squandered, for telling stories that perpetuate the Brand. However, to their credit, BlackBerry created a support program, called *BlackBerry Jam*, for people who develop applications for BlackBerrys. Then they came up with *Jam Sessions*, an initiative for developer collaboration. Beautiful. So why can't they come up with an enduring positioning statement – one more integrated than past attempts like *Love what you do, A bold enhancement* or *Act on inspiration*?

The name you want, even if it's a word you (think you) made up, is probably already in use by someone else.

Job 4: Be Distinct

Your Brand is unique. Your name should be too. So please don't add to the infinite number of names that copycat Apple's system of names starting with i. Same goes for anything ending in *-ia, -opia, -icious* or *-city*, which were inspired by the likes of *Expedia, Fruitopia, Bootylicious* and *Travelocity*, but have now been done. To death. They're just not differentiating anymore.

*It's what people think of you™

If you have any names like these on your shortlist, cross them out or risk sounding stale and contrived.

Fact is, distinctiveness is a seriously high bar when you consider that the name you want, even if it's a word you (think you) made up, is probably already in use by someone else. This could present legal issues if you operate in the same industry or jurisdiction as your twin, but the challenge is even greater than that.

For example, now that we have the Internet and Google, people will find out that your ad agency in Ohio has the same name as an ad agency in Alberta (one that might even rank higher than you in search returns). Ad agencies are supposed to be creative, and a name that isn't unique knocks your brilliance down a notch. Even if you're not in a creative industry, your thoroughly thrashed-out Brand Foundation is supposed to have a strong difference, which implies a different name.

Job 5: Be Memorable

It should go without saying that if people can remember your Brand's name, it will serve you much more effectively. The qualities that make a name memorable overlap with several of the other jobs – it needs to be remarkable, distinct and communicate the Brand Foundation, for example.

In addition, memorable names are almost always:

- Short (they have one, two, or three syllables)
- Meaningful (by conveying multiple layers of meaning)
- Easy to spell and pronounce
- Pleasing to the ear

And finally, memorable names definitely DO NOT have initials.

The Initial Mistake

Choosing a name with initials is a good way to make your life miserable. A set of initials has no personality, no emotion, no visual imagery and is very difficult – a pain, really – to remember. Rest assured you will end up constantly repeating and explaining your name to everyone who is trying to understand 1. What the heck it is and 2. What the heck it means.

*It's what people think of you™

Initial names are successful when earned, not created. So why do otherwise smart businesspeople slap initials on a logo and think their work is done? Because very successful companies like GE, BMW and UPS surround them. People see this successful Branding and think they can emulate it. What they forget is that companies like these have earned the right to use the short form. Often it was their customers who started using the convenient shorter version long before the Brand itself formalized the use.

Initial names are successful when earned, not created.

Of course, we all know that *GE* stands for *General Electric* and *HP* stands for *Hewlett-Packard*, because these Brands have been around forever and have spent infinite amounts of money to build awareness.

But please take a moment and tell me what these abbreviations mean:

- *AMD*
- *AME*
- *CNS*
- *FPL*

All of these are real organizations. But it's unlikely you have any idea who these Brands are or what they do, because unlike GE or HP, they have not spent billions, over decades, spreading the word.

Have you?

Keep it Short

Think of almost any well-known Brand name, and it will be brief – two or three syllables at most. If the Brand name you're thinking of is longer than three syllables, chances are very good that it's been shortened by customers or by the Brand itself – like *Federal Express* to *FedEx*.

Pick a short name for your Brand, or people will shorten it for you. And then you'll probably lose the meaning you worked so hard to convey.

*It's what people think of you™

Kinect

Kinect, the name of Microsoft's controller-free video game, conveys many layers of meaning in just two syllables. *Kinect* of course is derived from con-nect. It's a memorable association, because players are connected to Kinect in an entirely new way. They do not hold any kind of controller. The game console scans your body with an electric eye, and then your movements (say, the way you throw punches in Kinect's boxing game) are interpreted through your character in the game. Thus *Kinect* is also derived from *kinetics* – defined as "the branch of mechanics...concerned with the study of bodies in motion."

Kinect is also short. It is easy to spell even though it's misspelled. And like many of the world's most successful Brand names (think *Disney, Google, Kraft,* and *Toyota*), it sounds pleasant and powerful by beginning with a "plosive" letter (those letters including d, g, k, p and t).

Job 6: Inspire and Attract Stakeholders

Remember: when you're choosing a name, your feelings don't matter. The feelings of others? That's a different matter entirely. That's because great, remark-able names have the power to inspire and attract.

But it's tough to be attractive when you have a name like *Retirement Residences Real Estate Investment Trust* (or *Retirement Residences REIT* for "short"). This was the unfortunate label of a publicly-traded company with 25,000 employees and 240 properties throughout Canada and the United States.

Then they ceased being a REIT, so they needed a new name. It was a rare opportunity to rid the company of an ineffective name that everyone short-ened and no one outside the organization could remember. Most impor-tantly and worst of all, the name said absolutely nothing about why any child should entrust their aging and vulnerable parent to this company's care.

Yet this company did care, deeply, about its resi-dents. Their Brand position was expressed as *The pinnacle of caring.* They also had a positioning statement: *Enhancing lives.*

Very often, employees will at first hate their organization's new name. Peo-ple are very resistant to change, especially when it's forced on them. This is what we cautioned the company's CEO to expect. But when he announced

*It's what people think of you™

to staff that the company's new name was *Revera*, they cheered. Rooted in the Brand's reverence for human life, *Revera* was a clear celebration of what guided these caring individuals in their jobs every day.

Job 7: Leverage an Existing Naming System, or Create a New One

How will a new Brand name leverage and add value to the others in your portfolio? This is the fundamental question of Brand and naming architecture.

An effective architecture makes it easy for customers to buy from you – by making it easy for them to understand the value of each offering and the differences between them. For example, Apple's decision to name its tablet *iPad* leveraged the equity of a very well-established naming system – that of the *i*-prefix epitomized by *iTunes, iPod* and *iPhone*. By signalling to consumers that they should expect the same kind of magic as those products, *iPad* as a name saved Apple millions in marketing.

Great names also create a rich reservoir of future naming and storytelling opportunities. Winnipeg's decision to call its reborn NHL team the *Jets* (instead of the *Moose*) was crucial to honoring the club's legacy. It also created a flexible platform for telling the Jets' story long into the future. Consider what the Jets called the big party to launch their triumphant return: *The After Burner Social*. Perfect. What they'd call a Moose-themed party, we're not so sure.

Job 8: Be Workable into a Suitable Domain Name

As of 2012, more than 350 million URLs, or domain names, were registered, and the World Wide Web was growing by 150,000 domains every day. A considerable portion of these domains are owned by resellers whose reason for living is to extract big bucks from you. For these reasons, it is extremely difficult to develop a Brand name that: 1. Is available for sale; 2. Is available for sale at a price you can afford.

But don't get too stressed about it. It is not the job of the name to be available as an URL. Instead, it is the name's job to be at least workable into a suitable URL.

*It's what people think of you™

Even that challenge can be difficult. But a creative workaround can almost always be found. Porter Airlines, for example, decided to use *flyporter.com* when porter.com was unavailable. High-tech firm ReVera owns *revera.com*, so for Revera, we bought *reveraliving.com* – which, because it says something meaningful about the Revera Brand, might even be considered an improvement over *revera.com*. In similar fashion, Square, a payment system that allows anyone to accept credit card payments with their smartphone, uses *squareup.com* – a very clever call to action.

This may seem counterintuitive, but web addresses are becoming less important by the day. Most people will find you through Google (which processes 1 billion searches every day), not by typing domain names into their browser's address bar. If your website has a reasonably effective SEO (search engine optimization) strategy, you should be easily found.

Job 9: Pass Linguistics

It may seem obvious that being free from offensive or inappropriate meanings is a vital job. Yet there are many missteps. Just one example is the *Lumia* cellphone (by Nokia), which in Spanish slang means "prostitute."

It's always a challenge to develop a Brand name that won't offend or annoy at least one human being somewhere on this planet.

It is always a challenge to develop a Brand name that won't offend or annoy at least one human being somewhere on this planet. But your first linguistics checks should be done against your native language. Not only is there an infinite and growing amount of slang you probably don't know about, you simply never know how someone might interpret your potential name.

Or abuse it. Pretty much any Brand name can be distorted into a derogatory (and often accurate and funny) nickname. *Jet Blue*, for example, became *Jet FU* ("eff you") when a flight attendant told off a passenger and then went down the emergency slide with a brewskie in each hand. Then there is *Calpice* for a beverage sold in Japan, which has been distorted to "cow piss."

When it's all said and done, the best way to protect your name from abuse is to live up to its promise every day.

Shortlisted names that survive the native language check should then be checked, by a qualified linguistics firm, against other languages relevant to your target market. There is a good chance that one or more names will be disqualified at this stage, as was *Truis* in our process with Revera – *Truis* found to sound like the insulting "female pig" in French.

Job 10: Pass Legal

As we know, there is an excellent chance that one or more names on your shortlist are in use somewhere else in the world. So it can be a question of which names are least likely to attract a legal challenge from parties already using it.

Research in Motion, for example, named a new BlackBerry operating system *BBX* (incidentally, a meaningless name and a lost opportunity to say something about the Brand). They were sued by a company already using that name for a piece of software. RIM was forced to rename its operating system *BlackBerry 10* (another lost opportunity), and received a lot of negative press – a debacle they could have avoided with a simple Google search.

Any name on your shortlist should pass this standard: it should be distinct from all Brands within its competitive set, and distinct from well-known Brands outside its competitive set. If a Google search found *BBX* to be the name of a bicycle instead of a piece of software, the next step would be a formal legal check done by a trademark lawyer.

Ideally, *BBX* would have been just one name on RIM's shortlist. Hopefully, one or more of those names would have survived the legal check, and from those the final choice could have been made.

Once you make your final choice, start using it absolutely as soon as possible: date of first use is a critical factor in any trademark dispute that can still come your way. Then seek further protection by starting the process of registering the name as a trademark.

One Way Among Many

Great names can be a big boost to your bottom line: they convey the essence of your Brand story, thereby decreasing your reliance on other forms of marketing communication. Integral to this equation is the power of names to inspire employees – which, as we'll see in the next chapter, is one way among many.

*It's what people think of you™

[16] Inspire the Team

Building your Brand from the inside out is the best way to ensure that your employees will instinctively deliver it to the world.

Stan: "What do you expect, from the guy who stole a kid's bicycle when his truck broke down?

Chuck: "Borrowed. I borrowed it."

Tom Hanks as FedEx manager
Chuck Noland in the film *Cast Away*

Just as stories inspiringly convey essential Brand attributes to employees, so do a variety of other methods: from the straightforward to the ambitious, from the obvious to the ingenious.

Delivering the Brand

When you have 300,000 employees working around the clock – in 220 countries around the globe and high above it – it's not easy to reach your people with the Brand message.

But in cooperating with Hollywood in the making of the 2000 Tom Hanks film *Cast Away*, FedEx set a new standard for getting it done. Hanks plays a passionate FedEx manager who, right from the opening scene of the film, preaches and lives what the Brand is all about: "Relax, it's FedEx."

Cast Away was a hit at the box office and certainly entertained millions of folks that didn't work at FedEx. But make no mistake: FedEx executives were

targeting not only their actual and potential customers, but FedEx employees themselves. All over the world, the most passionate fans of the film are the employees of the gigantic overnight package mover, who share the movie so family and friends can see and feel what FedEx culture is all about.

Those employees have every right to be proud. Heck, Hanks was stranded on a desert island for four years and still delivered the one remaining package from his ordeal.

Just imagine how inspiring *Cast Away* was to FedEx workers. The film is full of dialogue and footage that celebrates the company's Brand of legendary efficiency and commitment. Here's Hanks living the Brand while playing FedEx manager Chuck Noland, inspecting a Russian terminal in an early scene:

> **Chuck:** There's only one way. We have to work together. Every one of us depends on everyone else. If one package is late, we are all late. If one truck misses the deadline, we all miss the deadline. Let's start by taking a look around.

And then:

> **Chuck:** Here, this table is too far from the wall. Packages can slip down...like... (pulls out a package from behind a table)...this. What could be in here? Let's say one of you sent it. Could be the closing papers on your dacha, could be a toy for

*It's what people think of you™

your grandson's birthday, could be a kidney to keep your mother alive. I don't think you want your mother's kidney to end up behind a table.

And imagine how much interest this film has inspired among friends and families of FedEx staff. "Is FedEx really like that? Do you think a FedEx worker would really deliver that last package the way Tom Hanks did?" I hope FedEx gave free *Cast Away* tickets to every single one of their employees and bought them the DVD to help spread the word.

Build Your Brand From the Inside Out

Seen from the perspective of FedEx employees, *Cast Away* demonstrates the common misperception that Brands target customers alone. In fact, by first focusing your Brand communications on internal stakeholders, you best ensure delivery of your Brand promise in that hyper-competitive world out there. In other words, Brands are built from the inside out. Because if you don't get your own employees inspired about your Brand, they sure won't be out there inspiring your customers at thousands of daily touchpoints.

Gerstner knew that if IBM was ever going to convince the market of the new Brand direction, he had to convince his own people first.

Convince Your Own People First

For *Cast Away*, maybe FedEx took a page from Lou Gerstner of IBM. Gerstner took over as CEO of "Big Blue" at a desperately bad time in the company's long history. In 1992, Interbrand's annual *Top 100 Global Brands* ranking put IBM's Brand equity at negative $52 million. That's right. It was calculated and determined that every time the IBM name was brought into the selling equation, it had a detrimental effect, resulting in negative Brand equity. That the Brand was worse than worthless.

Gerstner wanted to change the company's focus from hardware, like mainframe computers, to solutions like consulting. But IBM was a massive organization. How to communicate the new direction?

*It's what people think of you™

Gerstner commissioned a series of ads that featured real IBM employees. Published in the business press, they were deliberately targeted to inspire IBM workers – the "old guard" in particular – to convince them that the company had changed its approach, and that they too should adapt. Gerstner knew that if IBM was ever going to convince the market of the new Brand direction, he had to convince his own people first.

Hold Up a Mirror

But most of us don't have hundreds of thousands on staff, and Hollywood agents aren't knocking down our doors. Not a problem – there are plenty of affordable inspirational opportunities if you go looking for them.

Like what we did at GSW, a client and manufacturer of water heaters, eavestroughs and other products. The company had become so diverse that when I did a job there early in the new millennium, it had lost all sense of identity.

What we did at GSW was give the Brand its pride back. We conducted a ThinkAudit and realized that they were the oldest manufacturing business in Canada. These people were part of a legacy with very deep roots back to a pioneering spirit. Not only that, the company was still creating innovative processes. Hence the new positioning statement: *Manufacturing Pioneers Since 1847.*

We had a university professor write a history book of the company. It included all kinds of pride-inducing tidbits – like stories about areas of the existing plant that were original, dating all the way back to the company's inception. I have a copy of the book, and it's a great read, but the primary target audience was internal. Just like the IBM ads were aimed at IBM workers themselves, a copy of the GSW history was distributed to all staffers. It was like a mirror they could look in to rediscover who they were. Then they could relate the story to others.

John Barford, the majority owner of GSW at the time, sold the organization in 2006. In a meeting with potential buyers, John walked around the boardroom table and placed a copy of the book in front of each suitor. Needless to say they were impressed. This was a company that ultimately commanded a price proportional to its deep Brand equity.

*It's what people think of you™

Janitorial Splendor

In Chapter 9, I discussed our work with commercial real estate manager Oxford Properties, where our goal was to smash the traditionally adversarial relationship between landlords and tenants. One part of our plan was to celebrate the custodians who were so intensely proud of their fine buildings. These guys would get into good-natured arguments over who had the shiniest marble floors and the cleanest elevators.

So we ran magazine ads, targeted at Oxford employees themselves, that featured photos of these janitors and gave tribute to their customer care commitment. The ads also appeared right in the building lobbies, standing tall on easel signs for the thousands of building occupants to see each day.

Another way we changed the landlord-tenant relationship at Oxford was by changing the vocabulary. I think that "landlord," a term from feudal times, is one of the scariest words in the English language. So we discarded that term and started calling Oxford simply "Oxford." And of course they became the first commercial real estate company in North America to call their tenants "customers."

Create a Unique Vocabulary

Starbucks is another Brand that understands the power of vocabulary. To sell coffee at never-before-heard-of prices, they describe their coffees in never-before-heard-of terms, like "Grande," "Venti" and "Trenta." In the land of Starbucks, baristas don't pour a cup of coffee, they craft your custom drink. My favorite is a Grande Bold. For Andris it's a decaf, Venti, five-shot, half-full Americano. I asked Zoe at my local store for the most customized drink she could think of, and this is what she rhymed off: half-caf, triple, Venti, sugar-free vanilla, non-fat, extra-hot, no foam, light whip latte. One unique drink, no doubt.

POS

Southwest Airlines has not a single international flight, but still flies among the most passengers of any U.S. airline.

They celebrated their 38th consecutive year of profitability in 2010. One of the many reasons behind this astonishing record is the way they capitalize the "C" in "Customer" and the "E" in "Employee" to emphasize the importance they hold (and I'm sure you've noticed our nod to Southwest in the way we capitalize "Brand"). And the most important reason is "POS." POS is what their 37,000 employees deliver every day – Positively Outrageous Service.

Positively Outrageous Service is expected of everyone at Southwest, from CEO Gary Kelly, to the pilots, to the refueling crew. It's POS that inspires pilots to help flight attendants clean planes between flights, and gets them turned around at the gate in an unbeatable 20 minutes. It's POS that's landed this airline on *Fortune* magazine's list of America's Most Admired Companies every year since 1997. And it's POS that has inspired airlines like Jet Blue and WestJet to replicate (with high but not equal levels of success) the Southwest Brand model.

Positively Outrageous Service is expected of everyone at Southwest, from the CEO, to the pilots, to the refueling crew.

Southwest proves that inspiring your people to be Brand ambassadors creates a virtuous upward spiral of opportunities to inspire them even more. Here is a Brand so confident in its ability to deliver POS that it signed up with A&E to produce *Airline*, a reality TV show that exclusively covered Southwest Airlines and the many dramatic and sometimes funny things that happened in their world every day.

Airline

How many organizations do you know with the guts to let A&E run a prime-time show of their front line people: telling a lady she can't fly today because her cute little doggie isn't allowed on board? Telling a mob of customers they won't be going home tonight because of flight cancellations? Dealing with obnoxious customers – who are often drunk as lords?

Because of their commitment to POS, Southwest employees came through it all with grace and flying colors – a huge inspiration to their colleagues and a compelling reason for any viewer to try out the Brand. In fact, Southwest received an average 9% bump in online bookings every Monday night after the show aired.

The Perfect Segue

Here at Instinct we've created a bit of unique vocabulary ourselves. For example, before I coined the term, there hadn't been anyone called a "Brand Coach." "Executive coaches" and "business coaches," sure; "Brand guys," yes; but never a "Brand Coach." Putting two well-known words together for the first time created new meaning, making potential clients curious about what my firm could do for them. When someone asks me what I do, and I reply "I'm a Brand Coach" their interest tends to be piqued and the next thing they say is:

"What's a Brand Coach?"

And then I get to tell them. I have a 19-second elevator speech and a two-minute cocktail party speech always ready to go. I recommend that you and everyone in your organization have one as well. I'm always surprised at how few people can crisply explain what they do for a living and what value they and their organization provide. But it's a critical skill in a hyper-messaged world where first impressions and referrals count for so much.

The Brand Does Not Belong to the Marketing Department

If the marketing people at Nissan are waxing poetic that "everything we Shift we make better" while their customer service line is a literal wrong number, all the beautiful ads in the world won't save their Brand. And there's no point in the marketing department at Volvo walking the Brand talk while their dealerships are giving out corkscrews and exploding the coveted "safety" position.

By first building your Brand through internal inspiration, you will ensure the greatest returns when your Brand reaches the outside world. When your team is functioning cohesively as an inspired unit, all focused on the promise of the Brand, they will instinctively communicate its attributes outside the organization – and stakeholders will listen.

Brand: It ain't the logo*

*It's what people think of you™

[17] Stop Giving

Focusing your charitable
activities on a single cause
will help you face the complex
challenge of finding and keeping
employees and customers – by
telling them exactly what you
stand for.

"Many people despise wealth, but few know
how to give it away."

Francois de La Rochefoucauld

Stop.

Stop contributing something to every charitable organization that comes asking. Instead, focus on a single cause aligned with your Brand. Cause-related Branding allows you to make a meaningful difference in one particular area and get people thinking about you in a way that reflects the essence of your Brand as cemented in your Brand Foundation.

There are approximately 1,000,000 registered charities in the United States and more than 80,000 in Canada. They aggressively and expensively compete with each other for the same pool of dollars. If all companies simply focused their giving on a single cause, imagine the marketing dollars these charities could save.

Focus on a single cause. Explain your rationale to all stakeholders. When you're approached by other causes, you can explain your focused approach and say "no" with polite justification.

Pro-Bono Branding

Charities don't just compete for donor dollars, they have a very tough time finding enthusiastic and talented volunteers and board members. So at Instinct, our single cause is not a particular charity, but the charities that need to understand what a Brand is, and how to build one in a disciplined way. These organizations, who have to make the most of shoestring budgets, can frankly have brutally bad Brand discipline.

A charitable giving approach that's aligned with your Brand will help you find and keep the best employees, and connect with customers.

We work with a select few and provide Brand Coaching on a pro-bono basis to their leadership teams and board members – all in direct alignment with our vision (*To be recognized as the organization responsible for teaching the broader understanding and value of "Brand"*).

Two Huge Challenges

A focused charitable giving approach that's aligned with your Brand will help you address two huge challenges faced by every organization. The first challenge is finding and retaining staff. The skilled labor shortage in the United States and Canada will continue to worsen. Attracting and keeping great employees will soon become the number one issue facing business.

The second challenge is finding and retaining customers in a world of hyper-messaging. A well-articulated Brand can give you a leg up on the competition by helping potential and actual stakeholders – customers, employees, investors, donors and volunteers – understand, identify and ultimately connect with your organization for reasons often more compelling than the almighty dollar alone.

Cause-related Branding is an especially powerful way of getting employees and customers to connect with your organization. It not only makes you feel great, it makes people feel great about working with you and for you. Your customers will understand and appreciate an organization that supports a good cause. And those soon-to-be-even-scarcer good employee candidates will warm to an organization that puts its money where its mouth is.

The Audacious Richard Branson

In 2006, concern about global warming was reaching a fever pitch. Virgin Group PLC chairman Sir Richard Branson, never one to miss a Branding opportunity, offered a prize of $25 million to the first person or group to develop a means of removing greenhouse gases from the atmosphere. This was a follow-up to his commitment the previous September to donate a whopping $3 billion toward the global warming fight. In a truly remarkable move, Sir Richard promised to direct all profits made in the next 10 years by his travel companies, including Virgin Atlantic Airways and Virgin Trains, toward the $3 billion donation.

In vintage Branson style, both donations fit the Virgin Brand – audacity – perfectly.

*It's what people think of you™

Lululemon and Empowerment

Red-hot Lululemon Athletica supports causes at both the local and national level. Brilliantly reinforcing its Brand message of empowerment, the athletic-wear company lets its customers decide which charity their local store should support. Nationally, Lululemon drives home its mission to provide *components for people to live longer, healthier and more fun lives* – by supporting Olympic rower Silken Laumann's Active Kids Movement[22], an organization that promotes unstructured play by children, and the Centre for Integrated Healing[23], a non-profit that provides integrated cancer care for people with cancer and their families.

Junk and Women's Health

1-800-GOT-JUNK? is another example of meaningful alignment between Brand and cause. It has aligned with Yard Sale for the Cure[24], an annual fundraiser for breast cancer research and treatment, that stockpiles donations from messy basements and garages. On the day of the big event, JUNK? runs its own gigantic sale and donates the proceeds. The alignment between 1-800-GOT-JUNK? and Yard Sale for the Cure works because breast cancer is obviously an important issue for the Brand's primarily female target market.

Southwest and "LUV"

The primary corporate charity of Southwest Airlines is the Ronald McDonald House program[25]. Inspired by a pilot whose daughter stayed at a Ronald McDonald House while being treated for leukemia, Southwest adopted the charity in 1985. Every year, the company – often referred to as "the Airline that LUV built" – sponsors LUV Classic golf tournaments whose proceeds go to the charity. This focused approach has enabled them to make a significant impact: the tournaments contributed more than $11 million by the initiative's 25th anniversary.

Strategic Philanthropy

Can cause-related Branding actually serve the corporate bottom line and do social good at the same time[26]? As part of considering this question in *Harvard Business Review*, business strategy icon Michael Porter noted that some corporate giving is just a barren exercise in self-serving PR. As an example: cigarette maker Philip Morris, who in 1999 gave $75 million to charity and spent $100 million on an ad campaign to publicize it.

The substance of Porter's argument, however, was that if a corporation's philanthropic efforts are to have meaningful bottom line and social effects at the same time, those efforts must improve the "competitive context" in which the company operates.

Porter cites the "strategic philanthropy" of Cisco Systems, DreamWorks and others. Cisco was hampered by a lack of qualified network administrators available for hire. So they launched the Cisco Networking Academy[27]. In cooperation with the United Nations, more than 9,000 academies have been established in 165 countries around the world.

Obviously all academy students don't go to work at Cisco. But the company provides itself with a tailored pool of talent to draw from, and people in need get the opportunity for a better future.

DreamWorks is the film studio behind the animated *Shrek* movies, along with live action Oscar-winners like *American Beauty* and *A Beautiful Mind*. Similar to the Cisco approach, the company trains low-income Los Angeles students in the specialized skills demanded by the film production industry[28].

Tap the Power of Branding

The world of registered charity is one of the most competitive environments for dollars there is. The big money makers are lotteries, gala events and the ubiquitous "walks" and "runs."

The result? An already massive competition for funds is further focused on relatively few event types. So hats off to the smart folks at Toronto's Princess Margaret Hospital Foundation[29] and their annual "Weekend to End Women's Cancers." They've tapped into the Branding discipline of differentiation to stand out from the crowd.

What's uncommon about their walk is the requirement that each participant raise a minimum of $2,000, a lofty sum – considering most participants in other walks raise not much more than the entry fee (somewhere in the neighborhood of $50 – $200). By setting this benchmark, Princess Margaret effectively hand-picks and energizes their walkers, limits their costs and maximizes their net revenue, which between 2003 and 2011 totalled – wait for it – *more than $100 million*. The Foundation advises that these funds have enabled numerous advances in cancer research and care.

Absolutely brilliant.

Rethink Breast Cancer

In the world of fundraising for breast cancer awareness, research and treatment, Amanda Blakley is someone who's taken Brand differentiation to a whole new level. Her best friend, age 23, was diagnosed with stage four breast cancer. Amanda's response was to build awareness among, and raise funds from, a younger group than typically attends cancer-fighting fundraising events. What better way to differentiate her brainchild than give it a fun, hip name like "The Booby Ball"?

Amanda's annual Booby Ball has been rolled into Rethink Breast Cancer[30], a charity that takes a "bold, enterprising and entrepreneurial approach" to helping "young people who are concerned about and affected by breast cancer." A hallmark of Rethink's differentiation strategy is the way they name events. Along with the Booby Ball there is the annual "Breast Fest Film Festival," the world's first film festival dedicated to breast cancer awareness.

Connect Wisely

Charities – just like for-profit goods and services – must stand out if they are to be noticed. If you work with a charitable organization, differentiate. Uncover a unique position, be the first to bring it to market and then stick with it. Set big goals so that internal people can really get their hearts into it. Then lead them with passion and purpose.

When organizing events, select your participants wisely. Target your niche carefully and connect with them completely. Ensure you can provide them with an experience worthy of the time, money and effort they are contributing.

*It's what people think of you™

If you're a for-profit Brand, aligning your charitable activities with your Brand Foundation organizes all stakeholders behind the cause. Employees are proud of what their organization does, and customers are proud to do business with it. In the minds of other targets – potential employees, customers, donors, investors and the media – the Brand's position is made all the more clear.

Brand: It ain't the logo*

*It's what people think of you™

[18] Mine the Equity

Many of the strongest Brands
hold out their heritage with pride.
But due to panic, neglect or the
passage of time, too many Brands
deny their full potential by
ignoring their history.

"The psychological importance of heritage
may derive from...a link to immortality."

Jack Trout
From *Differentiate or Die*

Honda's outboard motors for powerboats have been leaders in environmentally-friendly technology since the 1960s. By the 1980s, their motors met California's *2006* emission standards, notably some of the most stringent in the world.

But you wouldn't have known it. Because Honda didn't tell anyone about it. It's just one startling example of many Brands that have passed on the golden opportunity to powerfully own a difference on the basis of heritage.

Like the Exxon Valdez. Just Bigger.

We had Honda as a client in the 1990s and demonstrated that competitors' engines were dumping the equivalent of (imagine!) two Exxon Valdez's into the freshwater lakes of North America every year. Competitors' outboards mixed oil into the gas, with the result that the oil was blown through the motor and right into the water. That was the standard technology at the time.

Honda, and no one else, was using a car engine in its outboards. Car engines lubricate without emitting oil – it's retained within the engine, not shot into the lake. But we couldn't convince Honda to tell the story of their environmentally-friendly heritage because they found it hard to look at themselves as anything but an engineering company. They liked their promotional materials full of charts and diagrams, not fluffy messages about preserving the environment.

The rest, as they say, is history. Little did Honda know that environmental preservation would finally emerge as a passionate consumer concern by the first years of the new millennium. But by then, Honda's advantage was gone. The entire outboard world had adopted engines conforming to the high standards initiated by Honda 40 years before.

Adi Dassler

 Adidas didn't suppress its heritage like Honda did, but rather dumped it in a panic about Nike's meteoric success in the 1980s. Adidas had been wildly popular in the 1960s and early 70s. It was *the* sports shoe and sportswear Brand and probably had market coverage just as broad as Nike eventually captured.

*It's what people think of you™

Adidas has a terrifically rich history behind its products. It was founded by Adi Dassler, a German shoemaker, in the 1920s. Dassler's vision was to create high-performance shoes for soccer and track and field. His shoes were first worn in the 1928 Olympics, but his big break came with Germany's victory over Hungary in the 1954 soccer World Cup. Germany's players were wearing Adidas soccer boots that, for the first time, had removable spikes.

But as Nike rapidly grew in the 70s, Adidas got scared. Nike had more of a fashion orientation. Adidas felt threatened by Nike's fashion-savvy approach and introduced new styles in the mid-70s that, incredibly, did not feature Adidas' iconic Three Stripes. Instead of sticking with its strength in soccer and track, Adidas tried and ultimately failed to compete with Nike in the arena of basketball shoes, where Nike managed to establish a dominant position that they still enjoy today.

The Adidas Mistake

Adidas made the mistake that many Brands make under pressure to meet new challenges presented by the market. They lose sight of who they are – and therefore how they can adjust their Brand strategy without throwing it out the window completely. Under pressure, Adidas jumped to the radical step of a Brand revolution.

What they should have done was take a simple evolutionary approach that wouldn't have sacrificed their hard-earned Brand equity. They should have worked twice as hard in the areas of dominance they already had. They should have shouted their soccer and track messages twice as loudly from the rooftops, instead of getting dragged off in a direction where they could not control the agenda.

The Three Stripes

I was privileged to work on the Adidas account in the 1990s. New ownership was in place that had the wisdom to take a fresh look into the company's heritage and rediscover the Brand's original focus on making a really, really good shoe targeted mainly at soccer and track and field. We brought back the Three Stripes identity that Adi Dassler had introduced in 1949, but had so foolishly been discarded by his successors. We used the Three Stripes consistently across all internal and external communications. We even reflected it in the architecture of their new headquarters, which included a track running through the center of the building. This concerted approach

*It's what people think of you™

led to a reversal of fortunes, making Adidas the fastest growing athletic Brand of the time.

Ford

I've always been dumbfounded that Ford doesn't do a better job of mining its Brand equity to establish a position that resonates powerfully with consumers. I mean, when you tell the story of the automobile, you start with Ford. They invented the category. The name of the guy running the company is right on the car. They used to have 100% market share. Who else has a story like that to tell?

Yes, it's true that Ford has started to rekindle America's love affair with the car. Some of this has been achieved by looking to the past – for example, by introducing a retro styling for their legendary Mustang. Fantastic.

They invented the category. The name of the guy running the company is right on the car. Who else has a story like that to tell?

The idea so connected with consumers that the other American automakers piled on. Chrysler copied Ford and brought out a retro-styled Dodge Charger. GM's Chevrolet followed suit with a redux Camaro.

But wait: rumor has it, Ford is going to change the Mustang *again* – to an "all-new, non-retro" design. What a horrible mistake. Message to CBO Mullaly: history works. At your fingertips are a bunch of great Brand positions to choose from: "being first," "invention," "innovation" or "pioneering" among them.

Buck-a-Beer

Earlier, I told the story of how premium beer-maker Sleeman forgot its rich heritage, trotted out the deck party ads and eventually slashed its prices to buck-a-beer. Just as Adidas was under pressure from Nike, Sleeman was being squeezed by a host of new entrants selling el-cheapo beer at a dollar a bottle. This was a deep discount from what Sleeman, a bona fide premium-quality brew, was charging – in the area of $40, not $24, for a case of 24. What did dropping from $40 to $24 do to Sleeman's margins? Ask Sapporo, the Japanese company that bought them.

Sleeman had a great Brand heritage to talk about, one that parlayed into a premium-tasting beer and ample justification to keep their prices where they were. Faced with buck-a-beer, their best strategy would have been to hold their prices firm – heck, raise their prices a tad – and tell people why their product was well worth it.

Stella and the Strong Brands

It's not like all of the other premium beers dropped their prices. Heineken, Stella Artois and other strong Brands held firm. But Sleeman, unlike these players, had lost its focus over the several preceding years and forgotten the Brand story they needed to withstand the cheap upstarts. John Sleeman was told by his new friends that the heritage angle wouldn't work with the young drinkers who were defecting to the cheapie beers. Nonsense. The stories about great-great-Grandpa Sleeman worked on young people in the 1980s and would work again. People of any age love to feel a connection with their history and demonstrate their sophistication by buying into it. Perhaps it's no surprise that Sapporo and John Sleeman have revived the beer's original heritage position. After all, Sapporo knows a thing or two about heritage themselves: they are Japan's oldest beer, founded in 1876.

Sadly, Sleeman is just one of a host of iconic Canadian Brands to falter and be purchased by foreign concerns since the 1980s. Labatt, Eaton, Hudson's Bay and Molson…all multibillion-dollar companies among the very oldest in North America, that played a key role in this continent's economic, political and social history. And in turn, each of them forgot their heritage and got bought out.

Tell Marketing it's Over

John Molson founded his company in 1786. It was a quintessentially Canadian organization (the flagship beer was called *Canadian*), and sometimes wore it proudly, to great effect. Take their invention of the "Joe Canadian" character in the 1990s and his "I am Canadian" rant. It's a campaign with a rock-solid position – patriotism – that's still talked about, still a part of the popular culture, years after Molson killed it off. Now they're owned by Coors.

There were three steps to Molson's Brand demise. Declining sales resulting from:

- The lack of a consistent Brand message;
- Brought on by a revolving door in the marketing department;
- All stemming from the dire need for a CBO.

Brands are built with consistency. Yet for years, Molson has used the marketing department as a training ground for more "important" management roles. And every guy who has ever come through this department has tried to make his unique mark to launch his important career.

Inside the Molson marketing department, it goes like this: question the old (maybe only eight-months-old) campaign idea and call the creatives at the agency (average business experience 3.5 years) to do something new. Or just hire a new agency and go from there.

Does anybody know what Molson brings to brewing, after 225 years? I don't think so. Every time someone abandoned an idea, they did the stakeholders a costly disservice by giving up Brand equity – the real value in companies today.

Pop Quiz: What's the Oldest Company in North America?

If you said the Hudson's Bay Company, you're right. The ultimate pioneers, they opened an entire new continent for business over three hundred years ago. Founded in 1670, by the 20th century they were only intermittently honoring their storied past. So they are no longer a quintessentially Canadian company, but an American one – owned by the Lord and Taylor department store chain.

Why wasn't the company consistent in using its rich history to build a killer Canadian Brand? Boredom. Generations of marketers at HBC were tired of hearing about the company's history all day long. In the hallways, they would walk by pictures of past chairmen – called "Governors" in company parlance – and shudder to hear about the "old days" or the company's crucial role in the opening of North America.

But the Americans have given HBC – the parent of the Bay department store along with Home Outfitters and Fields – its Canadian mojo back. And they're using HBC's history – hundreds of years of merchandising on a continent where it was tough for humans to survive, forget about build a business – to convey their right to be a great retailer.

*It's what people think of you™

They have resurrected the original coat of arms identity and are featuring the iconic green, red, yellow and blue stripes – made famous by the Hudson's Bay point blanket – much more. Exactly how embedded in North American history are those stripes? I am fascinated to note that they're present in the early history of Arizona, the state of my winter retreat, in paintings and other cultural media.

CBO Bonnie

At HBC's flagship Bay Brand, an aggressive repositioning is taking place. At department stores formerly known for scratch-and-save discounts, new CEO Bonnie Brooks is ending the practice of apologetic pricing. She dropped more than 200 so-so Brands and replaced them with a much smaller array of labels that people really want. Then she featured them in their own sections, store-within-a-store style, to give them prominence and, by extension, class up the Bay overall.

By featuring the stripes on an array of stylish items – some historic (scarves and the legendary point blanket), some new (snowboards and doggie clothing) – an old Brand has been made cool, and sometimes quite pricey, again. Epitomized by The Room, the ultra-upscale floor with jaw-droppingly rich prices on high-fashion clothing.

Embracing the role of CBO, Bonnie is touching every aspect of the Brand experience, even doing radio spots in her own voice. The messaging is directed at customers, sure, but it's equally targeted at her staff and key suppliers. Bonnie clearly understands the importance of getting every stakeholder to understand a new direction based on old history.

Jack Trout

Jack Trout is the genius behind the Branding bible *Positioning: the Battle for Your Mind*. In another of his fine books, *Differentiate or Die – Survival in Our Era of Killer Competition*, Trout tells readers that heritage goes deep into the soul of North Americans:

> The psychological importance of heritage may derive from the power of being a participant in a continuous line that connects one with the right to be alive, to a history that one carries forward from the living past – a link to immortality[31].

In the Bay's category, retail, there is one company that truly understands this power. It is none other than the behemoth of Bentonville, Arkansas: mighty Walmart. Everyone from sales clerks to top executives is immersed in the legend of Sam Walton, who began with a five-and-dime discount store and created the world's largest retailer by delivering the lowest prices, and as a result, better lives for his customers.

The Best Part

The greatest thing about an organization's heritage is that it's theirs alone. No two entities have the same past. A Brand's history is thus unique and ownable, two preconditions for any strong Brand position. Heritage represents a built-in, meaningful Brand just waiting to be leveraged. And in this day and age, getting and holding onto something meaningful is very, very tough.

[19] Protect Your Brand

Enlist yourself and those around
you to stay on the lookout for threats
to your Brand. And be sure to look
in the mirror.

"One of the things that we recognized...
was that probably of all of the assets on our
balance sheet, none was more important
than the brand, even though it wasn't
capitalized at all."

Fred Smith
CEO
FedEx

The New York Yankees in pink?

As one of the most valuable Brands in the history of sport, they, like so many other major sports organizations in recent years, have been playing fast and loose with their Brand identity. Check out their website and you'll see all manner of clothing items – baseball caps and jerseys, of course, but also everything from ladies' sleepwear to outfits for tots. In principle, I think that the merchandising is just great.

What I object to is the Yankees' world famous "NY" logo presented in pink and a variety of other colors that stray from the team's official logo shades of navy blue or white. I find it interesting that the Yankees would undoubtedly spend millions, at the drop of a baseball cap, to sue the pants off of another organization found to be stealing the NY logo, but that they pirate their own logo from within.

 The National Hockey League is especially guilty of self-piracy. Almost every team has a "third uniform" that presents their identity in a new and sometimes vastly different way than their perennial two designs: home and away. The Boston Bruins' third jersey, for example, discarded the classic "B" on the chest for the cutesy-poo face of a cartoon bear. And of course the Bruins, along with hockey Brand heavyweights Toronto Maple Leafs, Montreal Canadiens and others, turn their logo the requisite pink on women's clothing.

We live in an era of rampant merchandise knockoffs that cost U.S. companies $50 billion annually and account for an incredible 7% of all global commerce. Garment-makers are among the hardest-hit. Isn't the crook's job easier when no one knows what a Yankees logo can, and can't, look like? Don't you dilute the value of the Maple Leafs Brand when no one can say for sure what it is, and what it isn't?

The 9 Steps

Perhaps you've seen the humorous TV ads of Stella Artois demonstrating how cherished the amber liquid is – like the one with bank robbers who let their money go up in flames rather than extinguish the fire with the last bottle of Stella.

*It's what people think of you™

Stella has made the very protection of its Brand a key Brand attribute. It has certified a limited number of bars and restaurants – those that have committed themselves to honoring Stella's "9-Step Pouring Ritual" for its draft product – as "Gold Standard Establishments." The Pouring Ritual is serious stuff. It includes steps like The Purification, The Sacrifice and The Bestowal. No matter what establishment it is served in, Stella is always poured in "the Chalice," a distinguished-looking glass with a flat spot on the stem for your thumb – so you don't put your hand on the body of the glass, warming up the beer.

Stella further communicates its fanatical commitment to the Pouring Ritual through the Annual World Draught Masters Finals. This highly anticipated event brings together the best bartenders and beer connoisseurs from around the world to determine who has the Ritual perfected.

Stella has made the very protection of its Brand a key Brand attribute.

Canoe

There is a group of restaurants in the Greater Toronto Area that does a wonderful job of carefully protecting a fine dining experience for patrons. They are the Oliver & Bonacini establishments, including the ultra high-end, hugely profitable Canoe on the 54th floor of a downtown office tower. The Oliver & Bonacini Brand is all about focus on the joys of food and fellowship. So Peter Oliver and Michael Bonacini have, in their higher-end establishments, taken the simple yet very thoughtful step of asking all diners to kindly turn off their cell phones.

Another key attribute of the Oliver & Bonacini Brand is scrupulous attention to detail, like Peter Oliver's documented eagle eye for burnt-out light bulbs. Don't count on seeing one the next time you're in Canoe, or for that matter, any other sign of what I call "dead plant syndrome."

Be Opening Day Ready

Have a look around your office. Many of you have foliage that is withering or downright departed. I see it all the time when visiting prospective clients (because actual clients have to water their plants...it's in our contract). They're often in the reception area, right where visitors form their first impression of your Brand. It could very well be a symptom of a larger deterioration of your Brand's physical presence that represents your organization poorly – the tattered flag out front, the worn-down carpet, those paint chips on the wall, the disheveled visitor coat closet, the newsletter that used to go out every month but slipped by the wayside...

My most vivid recollection of dead plant syndrome is an experience at PICK-SEED, a client that supplies grass seed and related consulting services for golf courses, including one of the most celebrated 18 holes of turf on the planet – Georgia's Augusta National, home of the Masters. I went to PICKSEED's corporate headquarters for the first time and, naturally, expected that their lawn would be an immaculate thing of beauty. Instead I stepped out of my car to find a lawn that was, in the golfing vernacular, a dog track.

Remember these two facts: most websites are terrible, and before a client meets with you, they are going to visit your website.

Needless to say, I pointed out this disconnect and the lawn is now a stunning representation of the Brand's commitment to excellence. Did it help them land the job of seeding every field for the 2010 World Cup of Soccer in South Africa? You can be sure it didn't hurt.

I have no doubt their well-built website didn't hurt either. Remember these two facts: most websites are terrible, and before a client meets with you, they are going to visit your website. So you'd better have something good there. I can guarantee you that FIFA, soccer's premiere governing body, had a look at PICKSEED's website before meeting them.

Chances are you wouldn't tolerate a torn flag or a crummy lawn on the day you first opened for business. Why accept them now? Practice being opening day ready every day.

Pockets of Persistence

Yes, there are a multitude of factors that can easily drag your Brand off course, despite your very best intentions. Your crucial, formal Brand protection tools are your CBO and intense, never-ending focus on your Brand Foundation.

A vital but less formal kind of Brand protection is to be found in what I call "pockets of persistence." Pockets of persistence are occupied by the people in your organization who function as thought leaders and influencers. Identify these people in your business. Involve them right from the beginning of your Brand-building efforts. Solicit their input: leverage their familiarity with your Brand to ensure that it remains true to its essence. Deputize them to tell the Brand story to their co-workers, persuade others of its rationale, actively protect the Brand from erosion by co-workers who are not yet fully bought-in, and attest to the legitimacy of the Brand-building process.

The job ranks and pay grades of these influencers are irrelevant. What matters is that these key people clearly understand what the Brand is all about, are comfortable communicating their understanding to others – even in the form of constructive corrections – and that others will listen to them.

When we developed the 310-maxx customer service program at Oxford, the receptionist in one of their many offices turned out to be the most effective thought leader. Everything that happened in that office revolved around her, as is frequently the case for those in gatekeeper roles, like administrative assistants and office managers.

From the start of the Oxford Branding process, we formally involved the receptionist and a number of other thought leaders from across the enterprise, engaging their active participation and input on how 310-maxx should work. Their contributions were vital, and they naturally developed a sense of ownership over the program. When the time came to roll out service excellence in the form of 310-maxx to Oxford and their customers, the receptionist and other influencers were tremendously helpful in building understanding and acceptance that 310-maxx was a carefully thought out, sensible and bound-to-be-effective program – not a fad.

Pockets of persistence aren't just vital in the Brand's early days. They are crucial to upholding the integrity of the Brand on an ongoing basis. Properly-empowered thought leaders give their colleagues coaching on living the

Brand day-in and day-out. They help ensure that anything not aligned with the Brand Foundation isn't done. Give them a sense of ownership from the beginning of a Brand project and you've built-in a living, viral system of Brand consistency.

Remember, even if yours is among the very strongest Brands, 100% of your employees will turn over in the next 10 years. For most of you, your employee base completely turns over every two to five years. You need your thought leaders to begin a viral spread of Brand thinking that will live on in future generations. Get them started – now.

[20] Ride Your Brand Through the Storm

Consistently observing strong Brand discipline in good times will carry your Brand through heavy seas – provided your problems do not conflict with the heart of the Brand promise.

"If you run a crap company to begin with, you have no money in the emotional bank."

David Neeleman
Founder
Jet Blue

An ice storm hit New York's John F. Kennedy airport on Valentine's Day, 2007. It was the Wednesday preceding the President's Day long weekend in the United States. Airlines were grounded. But for the passengers of one particular airline, the storm was especially brutal.

That airline was Jet Blue Airways, a Brand with one of the very strongest reputations for customer service in an American industry extremely short on stars. It's been the subject of numerous case studies on effective Brand strategy and is known by people far and wide who've never even seen, much less traveled on, one of their planes. Their self-stated "simple goal" upon launching in 1999: "to bring humanity back to air travel."

Oops. A total of nine aircraft were stuck on the runway that Valentine's, far from the terminal, for up to eight hours. One of them carried "99 passengers...stuck for nine hours without food, water and clean bathrooms[32]". For reasons not at all clear, Jet Blue was unable to do so much as roll up some stairs and let these poor people – hungry babies and all – off the damn planes.

Jet Blue cancelled a total of 1,100 flights, messing up the travel plans of a whopping 130,000 customers and creating scheduling problems that were not resolved for several days afterward. Jet Blue founder and CEO David Neeleman was so swamped, he couldn't get loose to do damage control on TV for five days, when he finally appeared on various programs including CNN's *American Morning* and even *The Late Show* with David Letterman.

On Letterman, Neeleman was evasive. Letterman did his darndest – "I'm going to ask you for the third time" – to find out why Jet Blue did so much worse than all of the other airlines faced with exactly the same weather conditions. Neeleman just kept saying he was sorry, that he knew what the problem was and that he was going to fix it. His personal performance did not reflect well upon the Brand. To his credit, however, he announced Jet Blue's new "Passenger Bill of Rights" that provided customers with full refunds if stranded on a plane for three hours or more.

The day after Neeleman's Late Show appearance, Jet Blue stock fell 5%. Three months later, it was down 20%, and the board of directors removed Neeleman from the CEO spot, into the role of Chairman and out of the limelight. Analysts commenting on the story cited Neeleman's entrepreneurial brilliance in growing Jet Blue to one of America's largest airlines, but saw his change of role as an acknowledgement that the company had "reached a certain size where visionaries are being pushed aside and the hard-core operations guys are taking over[33]."

Problems like Jet Blue's can push a Brand into a death spiral. Key people inside the organization must be at their best in order to manage a turnaround. To help out, new executives and line workers often must be brought in from the outside.

Your Brand must be strongest when it is under the greatest threat. Imagine for a moment that Jet Blue, like most other airlines in the U.S., was not so strongly associated with outstanding customer service. That it had no substantial reserve of Brand equity in the minds of the current and potential employees who will be so vital to improving its fortunes. Imagine that for Jet Blue, the pool of top-notch talent dries up and their talented people start to leave. Now imagine how hard it will be for them to make a turnaround.

Your Brand must be strongest when it is under the greatest threat.

Trouble in the Wheelhouse

I asked in this book's first edition: Will Jet Blue survive? When it comes to controversy facing any organization, two simple questions apply. First, has the organization made a sufficient prior investment in its Brand – in the form of Chapter 1's consistency, management and time – to carry it through the storm? If they have, good. And second, is the challenge faced by the organization squarely in its wheelhouse, being the heart of the Brand promise? If it is, bad.

For Jet Blue, the answers were "yes" and "yes."

For a Brand that talks about bringing humanity back to air travel, the Valentine's Day debacle couldn't have been a more direct hit to the wheelhouse. But while Neeleman was certainly guilty of inadequate performance, he apologized profusely for all of the inconvenience, vowed to fix the problems and, finally, introduced the Passenger Bill of Rights.

*It's what people think of you™

I predicted in the first book that Jet Blue would rebound nicely, and that's how it looks. They are one of the stronger airline Brands in the United States, with a four-star rating on airlinequality.com, and were ranked 3rd out of 18 carriers in the 20th annual Airline Quality Rating.

Every Day Low Prices

 Walmart. Lots of people love them, lots of people hate them. They face strong opposition virtually everywhere they open up a store. Community groups take shape to protest their impending arrival. They're accused of killing downtown retail in smaller communities by obliterating competitors and paying paltry wages without benefits.

They're accused of union-busting – the first Walmart in North America to successfully unionize, in the province of Quebec, was promptly shut down by corporate office.

It's been said that getting a Walmart contract is the best thing, and the worst thing, that can happen to a supplier – because the Goliath extracts the lowest possible prices and enforces the strictest terms of trade.

With all of this opposition, Walmart grows ever-larger and more powerful. How do they do it? There are plenty of valid arguments to be made around their supply chain management and unprecedented economies of scale. But a Brand is what people think of you, after all. So the reason it all holds together is that an enormous number of people think positively about the Brand. And many of them want to work for it, too.

Walmart has been so consistent at communicating its low-prices/live better message and delivering on it, a few pesky protestors aren't about to take down the company. Because Walmart's behavior is in the name of keeping prices low, the public has been willing to excuse it.

Martha, Martha, Martha

 Being bad obviously hasn't hurt Martha Stewart, either. In 2002, the year that allegations against her of insider trading broke, the stock price of Martha Stewart Living Omnimedia was as high as $19.40. In 2004, the year of her conviction for obstruction of justice (and her trip to "Camp Cupcake"), the stock went as high as $29.00, an increase of 49%.

*It's what people think of you™

Her customers, almost all women, don't care that Martha Stewart was a jail-bird, because everyone knows in the first place that Martha Stewart is an unpleasant person. Her Brand is all about making the perfect home for your family and guests. Her indiscretion has nothing to do with that.

All Brands Trip

Eventually, all Brands trip. The cause could be a general recession, industry-specific weakness, intense competition, poor Brand management, unforeseen events or outright malfeasance. Whatever the scenario, budget cutbacks are often required, and it's practically a given that marketing expenses get the scissors first. Hence there is less money and resources available to send out the Brand message through paid communication channels.

In the economic downturn of the early 1990s, both General Electric Appliances and Maytag had to cut back drastically on advertising and promotion. GE restricted its communications activities to brochures and dealer displays. Maytag bought a plane ticket.

They sent the Maytag Man, played at the time by Gordon Jump of *WKRP in Cincinnati*, on the road for a multi-city promotional tour. In Toronto at the super-sized Eaton Centre, he had people lined up the length of the mall just to get his autograph, was featured on the evening news and even made the front page of every major newspaper.

Maytag faced the same tough economy as GE. Maytag's higher degree of concentration in the big ticket consumer durables market made them just as vulnerable to recessions as GE, maybe more: because a relatively pricey washing machine is something you might put off buying when money is tight – say, compared to buying a light bulb or microwave. To boot, the recession included a downturn in new housing starts, again a factor supposedly more negative for Maytag than highly diversified GE.

Why was the Maytag Man's tour so successful? Chalk it up to the decades-long stamina of the Brand to stick with its Lonely Repairman, the pillar of their Brand position at the time. Maytag's wonderful consistency up to that point earned them a reservoir of Brand equity that allowed them to keep Brand expenses low and awareness high at the same time – allowing them to ride the Brand through the storm.

Ol' Lonely?

In this book's first edition, I said this about Maytag:

It's especially interesting that Maytag has retained its extraordinary Brand equity for so long when you consider a growing chorus of complaints that product quality has really taken a nosedive. As you might have guessed, I have a Maytag washer. I had a repairman come by recently (not the Maytag Man...'Ol Lonely doesn't work in cottage country north of Toronto) and he mentioned that the washers are becoming notorious for substandard quality. Apparently 'Ol Lonely isn't so lonely after all.

But, judging from the media's unanimous gushing over the recent contest to select the new Maytag Man, you would never know that Maytag is having quality problems. That's what years of fighting off old and new friends can do for a Brand. Maytag clearly has to fix its quality issues. Giving them the time they need to straighten things out, however, is their magnificent consistency at communicating the dependability message.

Maytag: your time is now up. I continue to hear your washers are poorly made and have ongoing maintenance issues. There is now a critical mass of consumers that recognizes your Brand position as illegitimate, and the Maytag Man – very sadly – as a joke.

[21] Make Them Want You

The most underused capability
of Brands is also the most promising
for the future: their ability to attract
and keep the people you want most,
and filter out those you don't.

"Your brand is your culture."

Tony Hsieh
Founder
Zappos

There is an exciting new frontier for Brands that I think will be the most critical for your business in the coming years. It is their power to attract and retain the best employees in the face of a labor crisis that is already gripping North America.

As discussed in the opening chapter, a smaller-than-ever cohort of young people is entering our labor market just as our workforce is aging like never before. These young people, the Millennials, look for meaning in their work to a degree considerably greater than previous generations. Making the situation even more difficult for employers is our continuing transition to an information-based economy, and the increasingly high levels of job mobility this shift gives to knowledge workers.

Attracting and retaining the best employees is a matter of communicating, through the Brand Foundation, what your culture is.

The Brand Foundation Filter

We know that a Brand isn't just a logo, website or advertising. And that the only synonym for "Brand" is "culture." Attracting and retaining the best employees is thus a matter of communicating, through the Brand Foundation, what that culture is. You have to tell your employees, over and over again, how their everyday work contributes to fulfilling the Foundation. Communicate in person and by proxy – by posting the Foundation on your website and office walls for all to see.

Present it when talking to new hires and new prospects: it will speak volumes about who you are. If it resonates with them, it will allow them to connect with your culture. If they're not enthused about it, you'll notice, and pass them by – or they'll realize it and look elsewhere. With the massive costs that go into hiring, training, retaining and terminating people, this should be an extremely attractive proposition to you.

You know Kyu Lee as the true CBO leader of QUEUE, the IT company with a Brand position of *Extraordinary service experiences*. As the final interviewer of potential employees, Kyu uses the Brand Foundation to great effect.

*It's what people think of you™

He tests candidates on their knowledge of Brand, both that of QUEUE's and the concept generally. He asks what they think makes QUEUE different – to see if they did their homework by reviewing the company website (where the entire Foundation is displayed). Kyu especially watches to see if candidates cite the company's extraordinary service levels. He also asks them to talk about something extraordinary they've done in life. If they pass the interview, they are walked through the Brand Foundation, officially, on their first day of training.

The bottom line is that Kyu wants new employees to thoroughly understand what "extraordinary" means at his company. Getting employee buy-in is essential – because the grind of daily details can blind anyone to a higher, motivating reason to put in their best every day.

Like Virgin

When you have 50,000 people in your 300 companies worldwide, employee motivation is a crucial concern indeed. Such is the case for Sir Richard Branson, Chairman of Virgin Group. In fact, he sees employee satisfaction as the very first order of business:

> Convention dictates that a company looks after its shareholders first, its customers next, and last of all worries about its employees. Virgin does the opposite. For us, our employees matter most. It just seems common sense to me that, if you start off with a happy, well-motivated workforce, you're much more likely to have happy customers. And in due course the resulting profits will make your shareholders happy.

Branson, of course, also believes very strongly in preserving the environment. All profits from his travel companies (Virgin Atlantic Airways, for example) are directed toward the now $25 billion he has pledged to fight global warming. The Virgin Group vision captures Branson's passions for people and the environment: *To contribute to creating happy and fulfilling lives which are also sustainable.*

A Social Mission

There is a chance, especially if you're in the corporate world, that this kind of lofty statement seems naïve to you. Maybe you don't think it is the role of business to make people happy and save the planet. In Brand Foundation sessions, I've seen CEOs scoff at the idea.

But listen for a moment to the CEO of a company with more than 800 million customers: Facebook. While preparing for his IPO, with mega-billions on the line, how does Mark Zuckerberg inspire the confidence of potential investors? He writes them an audacious letter reframing shareholder value:

> These days I think more and more people want to use services from companies that believe in something beyond simply maximizing profits.

And:

> Facebook was not originally created to be a company. It was built to accomplish a social mission — to make the world more open and connected.

The Kinross Way

If you're still skeptical, just know that with people like Zuckerberg leading the way, a commitment to something beyond money is an unmistakable trend among some very serious people in some very serious organizations.

Organizations like Kinross Gold, a multibillion-dollar, publicly-traded mining company. Because university mining programs are rare, there is a chronic shortage of graduates, and Kinross has to compete aggressively for them.

 Enter The Kinross Way, the guide that describes the Kinross culture to potential employees and other stakeholders. The pillars of The Kinross Way are the Brand's values. The first two are *Putting people first* and *Outstanding corporate citizenship*. Then there is *Rigorous financial discipline* and *High performance culture*. It adds up to a high-minded yet balanced approach that attracts top graduates to Kinross and has led to some wonderful examples of environmental preservation.

Case in point: Kinross took over a mine at Kettle River-Buckhorn, in the state of Washington, after two previous companies couldn't get the mine up and running because they couldn't meet environmental requirements. Kinross not only got the mine going, they developed it so carefully that water leaving the site was cleaner than when it arrived.

Making it Happen

To be effective, The Kinross Way or a Brand Foundation has to be more than just words on paper. If you want to attract the best and keep them, it has to be the starting point for delivering the culture you promised. Policies, processes and procedures have to be established to make that happen.

*It's what people think of you™

They don't have to be complicated. At Virgin, staff are encouraged to demonstrate "Virgin behaviors" and are rewarded for providing service over and above customer expectations. The company also applies this principle to its recruitment process, seeking to recruit "Virgin people" instead of focusing solely on who can do the job from a skills perspective. Like millions of organizations around the world, Virgin has an annual event celebrating the Employee of the Year, and there is ongoing recognition through "Stars of the Month" initiatives.

You are Not Boring

But what if you aren't a celebrity CEO, or sending a man to the Moon, or building cars that don't hurt anyone?

You might think that your business is mundane – that it serves no glorious higher purpose – but I say nonsense. I once told a company that imports industrial rubber: "You've got to be able to say that this piece of rubber can save America!" Because I'm convinced it was one very important piece of rubber. This company got it – and is now refocused and re-energized around their new core purpose: *To make the world a better place.*

[A] Afterword
by scott chapman
chief brand officer, managing partner of instinct brand coaches

Several years ago, I cut short a career at PepsiCo to join Instinct because I wanted to make a significant positive impact on our society. I had met Ted Matthews and quickly appreciated his inspiring and relentless passion for building strong and lasting Brands. Ted also made me realize the importance of powerful Brands to ensuring the continued prosperity of North American society. And so I knew that as Brand Coaching was Ted's life's work, it would also become mine.

Now as Chief Brand Officer and Managing Partner of Instinct, I am picking up the mantle from Ted and what he started more than 10 years ago with the founding of Instinct.

My request of you is to join me in championing our core purpose – *To advance the sustainability of North American organizations, reinforcing our free enterprise system and continued prosperity as a society.*

North American society is on the brink. With the erosion of our manufacturing base, the unprecedented amount of messages bombarding us every day and the worsening labor shortage, North American organizations and Brands are challenged like never before.

And according to Deloitte, happiness is at an all-time low, with 80% of people disliking what they do for a living. Happiness matters – because, as the Gallup-Healthways Well-Being Index reports, a happy workforce in the U.S. alone could increase productivity by $300 billion every year.

Instinct's proposal, as argued in this book, is that we must learn from and revitalize the instinctive ability and sense of purpose entrepreneurs have demonstrated in leading their Brands – and by extension, our economy – to prosperity over the past century. This very powerful phenomenon, which we call Instinctive Brand Leadership™, is based on the entrepreneur's instinctive understanding of what a Brand really is and what we all must embrace – that a Brand is what people think of you.

In organizations with this understanding, Brand drives every goal, informs every decision and shapes every message. It is understood by all departments, and people in all roles. In other words, it is the culture of the organization – "culture" being the only synonym for "Brand."

When you start to think of an organization's Brand as its culture, you start to understand why Brand matters for every type of organization – B2C, B2B, not-for-profit and government. And when properly understood and leveraged, the Brand has proven to be an organization's greatest value creator.

The bottom line: we are entering a new era that requires a different way of thinking about exactly what value, in human terms, we are contributing to society. Entire communities, families and our society at large depend upon our collective ability to embrace the right definition of Brand and fully leverage its potential. Whether you're an entrepreneur attempting to get your new idea off the ground or a professional manager at a Fortune 500 firm, there is nothing more important you can work on today than building your Brand.

Instinct is thrilled to participate in the publication of the refreshed version of *Brand: It ain't the logo* (*It's what people think of you)*. In the time since the original book was published in 2007, it has made frequent appearances on the *Globe and Mail's* business bestseller list. This has made us humbled and at the same time proud as an organization – and reaffirmed to our team that our Brand-building discipline is gaining traction and appreciation in the marketplace. And now, in alignment with Instinct's mission – *To support and challenge leaders to maximize the potential within their Brand* – an update and relaunch of the book can only serve to reinforce, even more strongly, the Brand Coaching work we do every day.

Scott Chapman

scott chapman
chief brand officer, managing partner
instinct brand coaches

www.instinctbrandequity.com

Core Purpose – *Why we exist.*

To advance the sustainability of North American organizations, reinforcing our free enterprise system and ensuring our continued prosperity as a society.

Vision – *Where we are going, and how we'll know we're there.*

To be recognized as the organization responsible for teaching the broader understanding and value of "Brand".

Mission – *What we do every day to get there.*

We support and challenge leaders to maximize the potential within their Brand.

Values – *What we believe in; our principles.*

We believe in doing meaningful work and living a meaningful life.
We believe in entrepreneurialism to drive the future of our society.
We believe 'Brand' has the potential to be an organization's most powerful value creator.
We approach every interaction with professionalism, integrity and precision.
We value long-term relationships.

Character – *How we act; our voice.*

Inspiring   Inquisitive
Disciplined   Knowledgeable
Brutally honest   Humbly brilliant
Fun

Position – *How we make a difference.*

Brand Coaching

Positioning Statement – *How we say our difference.*

A Brand is what people think of you.™

[C]   Ted's Maxims

Old friends are a Brand's worst enemies. New friends are the next worst. 14, 15, 50, 51, 52, 53, 56, 60, 74, 105

Branding is not a matter of personal taste. 22

Being consistent is the number one rule of Branding. 23, 48, 50, 53, 74, 113

The only synonym for "Brand" is "culture." 28, 69, 82, 190, 195

Brands are tools of self-defense. 33, 42, 113

Think "fresh," not "new." 55, 57

Just when the people inside your organization are getting bored of your Brand message, the target market is just starting to notice it. 57

Evolution, not revolution. 98, 99, 101, 102

Branding is a process, not an event. 107, 108

The only thing harder than building a Brand is changing one. 108

Branding is not an event – but losing one often is. 110

Brands are built from the inside out. 111, 155

Initial names are successful when earned, not created. 147

Dead plant syndrome: the neglected details that say so much. 179, 180

Be opening day ready everyday. 180

Create pockets of persistence. 181

Your Brand must be strongest when it is under the greatest threat. 185

[D] Endnotes

Chapter 3 – Be Remark-able

1   Godin, Seth. Purple Cow: Transform Your Business by Being Remarkable.
New York: Penguin Books Ltd., 2003.

Chapter 5 – A Brand's Worst (and Next Worst) Enemies

2   http://www.cbsnews.com/8301-505123_162-42740665/arnells-explanation-of-
failed-tropicana-design-resembles-his-nonsensical-pepsi-document/

Chapter 6 – Build a Foundation

3   http://www.ted.com/talks/lang/en/simon_sinek_how_great_leaders_inspire_ac
tion.html

Chapter 7 – Be the CBO

4   John P. Kotter. "Leading Change: Why Transformation Efforts Fail."
Harvard Business Review, March-April 1995, 59-67.

5   Ibid., 64.

6   Hawn, Carleen. "If He's So Smart...Steve Jobs, Apple, and the Limits of Innovation."
Fast Company, January 2004.

7   "Triumph of the Nerds: The Rise of Accidental Empires" (1996).
Made-for-television documentary.

Chapter 9 – Listen to Your Stakeholders

8   Wylie, Ian. "Talk to Our Customers? Are You Crazy?"
Fast Company, July/August 2006, 70.

Chapter 11 – Branding is a Process, Not an Event

9   http://www.consumerfreedom.com/news_detail.cfm/headline/2768

10 Zyman, S. The End of Advertising As We Know It.
Hoboken, NJ: John Wiley & Sons, Inc., 2002.

Chapter 12 – Deliver Great Experiences

11 Gerber, Michael E. The E-Myth Revisited: Why Most Small Businesses Don't Work
and What to Do About It. New York, NY: HarperCollins Publishers, 1995.

Chapter 13 – Make the Story Live and Breathe

12   Lukas, Paul. "The Great American Company."
     Fortune Small Business, April 2003, 24-28.

13   Ibid., 36-42.

14   Ibid., 44-49.

15   Ibid., 90-93.

16   Grubbs-West, Lorraine. Lessons in Loyalty: How Southwest Airlines Does It
     – An Insider's View. Dallas, TX: CornerStone Leadership Institute, 2005.

17   www.google.com

Chapter 14 – Be the Mythographer

18   Pink, Daniel H. A Whole New Mind: Why Right-Brainers Will Rule the Future.
     New York, NY: Riverhead Books, 2005.

19   Ibid., 103.

20   Ibid.

21   Ibid., 108.

Chapter 17 – Stop Giving

22   http://www.silkensactivekids.ca

23   http://www.healing.bc.ca

24   http://www.yardsaleforthecure.com

25   http://www.rmhc.com

26   Porter, Michael and Mark R. Kramer. "The Competitive Advantage of Corporate
     Philanthropy." Harvard Business Review, December 2002, 57-68.

27   http://www.cisco.com/web/learning/netacad/academy/index.html

28   http://www.dreamworks.com

29   http://www.pmhf-uhn.ca/Pages/Home

30   http://www.rethinkbreastcancer.com

Chapter 18 – Mine the Equity

31   Trout, Jack. Differentiate or Die: Survival in our Era of Killer Competition.
     New York, NY: John Wiley & Sons, Inc., 2000.

Chapter 20 – Ride Your Brand Through the Storm

32   http://www.usatoday.com/travel/flights/2007-02-20-jetblue-bill-rights-fliers_x.htm

33   Schlangenstein, Mary, and David Mildenberg. "Jet Blue Replaces Neeleman at
     Helm." The Globe and Mail, 11 May 2007, B8.

[E]   Index of Brands

About the Authors

ted matthews
brand coach, founding partner
instinct brand coaches

Ted Matthews may have persuaded adidas to bring back The Three Stripes and convinced Energizer not to kill the bunny, but as Canada's original and foremost Brand coach, he continually pushes his clients to understand that a Brand is not a logo, website or advertising. Instead, *a Brand is what people think of you™*.

As an entrepreneur, Ted built Promanad Communications into an 80-person firm that, over a span of 30 years, served an extensive list of blue chip clients. When it became clear that most professionals operate as if a Brand really *is* just a logo, he sold Promanad and founded Instinct Brand Coaches. Drawing on his own experience as a CEO, Ted teaches his clients to embed, throughout the organizational culture, instinctive behaviors that help their Brands earn a spot in the minds and hearts of increasingly discerning stakeholders.

Ted's dogged execution of the Instinct mission – *To challenge and support leaders to maximize the potential within their Brands* – has spurred some of the most successful Brand evolutions in North America. He has been an integral force behind the Brand-building efforts of organizations such as adidas, Manulife, Oxford Properties, Morneau Shepell, Strata Health, AtlasCare, Quadrangle, Revera, Advocis, IAMGOLD, Kinross Gold, PICKSEED, Investment Planning Counsel, Steam Whistle Breweries, ornge and Street Kids International.

For his pearls of wisdom and famously entertaining style, Ted is a sought-after speaker for business schools, corporations and professional associations. Helping lay the groundwork for future Branding excellence and building from his 18-year involvement with the Young Presidents' Organization, he also makes time to coach young entrepreneurs.

While Ted Brands himself a master woodworker, his wife Marsha is more likely to call it "making sawdust." The two live between the island cottage he built in Muskoka and the desert home they designed together near Phoenix.

About the Authors

andris pone
president, coin

Andris Pone is president of Coin, the Brand naming company. He has worked on naming assignments for major organizations including Scotiabank, Intel, AON, Morneau Shepell and Interbrand. Driven by the belief that names have jobs to do, his name portfolio includes *CDM Smith, KingSett Capital, Hotel Gelato, Revera, Myrex, Uprising* (for EllisDon), *Turnout* (for The National Ballet of Canada) and *LikeWise* (for Canadian Tire).

Other client work has included RPA, Fairmont Hotels & Resorts, Purolator, WPO/YPO and speaking engagements with leaders at Starbucks, The Home Depot, Unisource, Domino's Pizza and Dunkin' Donuts.

Andris serves on the board of directors of Epilepsy Toronto – the organizers of Scotiabank BuskerFest, which attracts one million people to Toronto's St. Lawrence Market each August. His not-for-profit work extends to a number of Branding initiatives at the Ontario Hospital Association, HealthAchieve, the Governance Centre of Excellence, Monarca and York Central Hospital.

Andris is often quoted in the *National Post*, has written opinion pieces for *Marketing* magazine and has appeared as a Brand expert on the Business News Network. He attended Saint Mary's University and graduated summa cum laude with a degree in Political Science. He also holds an MBA, with specializations in Marketing and Strategy, from the Schulich School of Business.

41805703R00115

Made in the USA
Middletown, DE
23 March 2017